Taking on the gods

Taking on the gods

The Task of the Pastoral Counselor

Merle R. Jordan

Wipf and Stock Publishers
150 West Broadway • Eugene OR 97401
2001

Taking on the gods

The Task of the Pastoral Counselor
By Jordan, Merle R.
Copyright©1986 by Jordan, Merle R.
ISBN: 1-57910-806-7

Reprinted by *Wipf and Stock Publishers*
150 West Broadway • Eugene OR 97401

Previously published by Abingdon Press, 1986.

Dedicated to Barbara,
who incarnates love and grace.

Acknowledgments

This book is implicitly the story of my journey, with its neurotic entanglements, idolatrous hang-ups, and redemptive moments, which has led me from devotion to false gods and to a false self to a gradually evolving awareness of the loving, validating God in Jesus Christ and to the resulting acceptance of the gift of grace and affirmation of my selfhood. A key life task for me has been to understand my history as an evolving spiritual journey out of which I can minister with empathy and love to other spiritual pilgrims. An entry in my personal journal from some years ago says: "My vocation is a ministry to interpret psychotherapy from a psycho-spiritual or operational theology point of view. It is to set the Christian revelation as the corrective world view to the distorted and self-destructive perceptions of the world, God, self and others which people have learned from authorities and sources which they have deemed to have ultimate significance. It is to address the transference distortions known as outdated maps of reality in the name of holy love as revealed in Jesus Christ."

I am deeply appreciative of those who have contributed to my journey and who have thus made this book possible. Perhaps my personal therapists across the years, men and women representing various schools of psychotherapy and religious traditions, have helped the most to transform some of my neurotic idolatry into redemptive loving. They have particularly impressed me as the flesh made Word. Clients have also been significant teachers as we journeyed together looking for more light in the darkness. Supervisees have been fun, challenging, and stimulating in discussions of clinical ideas concerning operational theology. Colleagues and friends have provided opportunities for mutual sharing, intellectual challenge, and emotional encouragement for my work in pastoral counseling.

I want to express particular gratitude to my colleagues at the Danielsen Institute and the School of Theology at Boston University, the staff at the South Shore Pastoral Counseling Associates, and to others such as Calvin Turley and Carroll Wright for their frontier exploration in operational theology. At various stages in the writing process Howard Clinebell, Howard Stone, and Ruth Cary have made valuable editorial suggestions. Friends from the religious community Wellspring in Gloucester, Massachusetts, suggested the title.

ACKNOWLEDGMENTS

While it is not possible to express appreciation to everyone who has contributed to my thinking, beliefs, and values over the years, and/or who has played a role in the preparation of this book, I simply offer my gratitude to those persons who have mediated such human/divine love that has creatively altered my beliefs, my life and my ministry of pastoral counseling. I thank my wife, Barbara, in particular, for her gracious love and her help in carving out the space necessary for this writing project. Finally, I thank Boston University School of Theology for the sabbatical leave which enabled me to focus on this task.

The language herein is meant to include both sexes, but unfortunately, some quotations may use exclusively masculine terminology.

Contents

Taking on the gods

Pastoral Counseling
as the Encounter Between Gods

> *Once you were ignorant of God, and enslaved to
> "gods" who are not really gods at all; but now that
> you have come to acknowledge God—or rather,
> now that God has acknowledged you—how can
> you want to go back to elemental things like these,
> that can do nothing and give nothing, and be their
> slaves? (Gal. 4:8-9 JB)*

Introduction

Despite its steady evolution, pastoral counseling
is still struggling to incorporate its primary discipline of theology into its clinical realities. Too often,
pastoral counselors have either become rigorously
psychological or operated from a purely religious
perspective. These counselors remind one of the
"Pennsylvania Indians who laboriously warmed
themselves for generations by fires of twigs, while

Acknowledgment is given to James Hagedorn for use of the phrase
"encounter between gods" taken from an unpublished article by himself
and the author.

15

camping for generations by fathomless beds of anthracite."[1] They have not mined the rich resources of a theological perspective in addressing the needs of their counselees.

Some pastoral counselors have clearly identified themselves as therapists utilizing no unique resources from their religious tradition to help their clients. Some specialists have even disavowed the ministerial tradition, with its paucity of helping resources, and have baptized secular clinical theory and practice as the way to "really help people." I have been at case conferences where the theological perspective was a victim of the "plop phenomenon." That is, the religious question or comment met with an embarrassing silence (plop) since the theological perspective was deemed irrelevant to clinical work. Charles Gerkin is correct to warn of the need to "offer an alternative to the absorption of pastoral counseling ministry into psychotherapy to the point of loss of the pastor's rootage in the Christian tradition and language."[2]

Ironically, while some pastoral counselors are rejecting their theological foundations, numerous secular therapists are turning to religious perspectives and spiritual resources in their clinical work. Major professional organizations are offering workshops and papers on various aspects of spirituality and religious meaning at their national and regional conferences. In a workshop on spiritual perspectives in psychotherapy that I conducted for the American Academy of Psychotherapists, one secular therapist stated the issue succinctly: "I am dealing so much with people's healthy and unhealthy religious experiences and belief systems in psychotherapy I feel at times that I ought to have theological training in order to do this work appropriately." This is an amazing change in the clinical world, to have some secular therapists experiencing themselves as amateur pastoral counselors needing theological perspectives and spiritual resources to meet their clients' needs.

This situation is reminiscent of the scenario in the 1950s when some parish clergy were giving up pastoral calling as an unrewarding and ineffective approach to ministry. At the same time, family therapists adopted this abandoned clerical activity and began visiting client families in their homes to observe them in their living environment. As home visits proved effective for family therapists, pastors returned full circle to their former views on the value of pastoral calling. Now there are hopeful signs that pastoral counselors are no longer waiting to utilize religious resources in understanding and helping others. Charles Gerkin has stated clearly that pastoral counseling is

> a process of interpretation and reinterpretation of human experience within the framework of a primary orientation toward the Christian mode of interpretation in dialogue with contemporary psychological modes of interpretation. The most basic tools of pastoral counseling are therefore seen as hermeneutical tools—the tools of interpetation. The pastoral counselor works self-consciously as a representative

of Christian forms of interpretation rooted in the primordial images of Christian understanding of the world. But the pastoral counselor, just because of his or her Christian orientation, comes at the interpretive task with profound respect for and hospitality toward the particularity of the experience of the individual sufferer. To represent the Christian mythos is not heavy-handedly to impose it. The hermeneutical philosophical tradition will be seen as offering ways of visualizing the encounter between the pastoral counselor as representative of Christian interpretation and the sufferer as interpreter of self experience that elucidates some of the nuances of that encounter across the boundaries of language and experience worlds. . . . In the world of psychotherapy, pastoral counseling asserts the normative value of Christian images of what human life under God was meant to become. Pastoral counseling is thus not only an important window to the world of theology, but also one of theology's best forms of Christian witness.[3]

Taking on the gods is a significant responsibility of pastoral counseling. Confronting those psychic structures, forces, and images which masquerade as God; bringing love, faith, and hope into the lives of persons; and being an extension ministry of Jesus Christ walking in the hells of human existence are all ways of expressing the true evangelistic purposes of pastoral counseling. The thought of taking on the gods in one's clients and in oneself may seem like arrogance or a humbling and awesome challenge. Nevertheless, taking on the gods is at the heart and soul of pastoral counseling.

Listening Perspectives

In the field of psychotherapy there are emerging what are called "listening perspectives" or orienting frames of reference.[4] I would like to stress the contribution of theology to the attainment of an accurate listening perspective. It is possible to miss significant meanings in clients' lives when such a theological listening perspective is not employed. As Lawrence E. Hedges puts it, therapeutic listening

> involves the attainment of a subjective grasp of the private experience of another person based on careful and empathic observation of that person's words and actions. Psychotherapists cultivate the art of listening because people feel they benefit from having their words and actions understood. Serious attempts to comprehend the private experience of others have given rise to many different ideas about the mind and its workings. Psychological theories are usually framed to focus attention on what we come to find are mental events, processes, structures, transactions and so forth. What often becomes obscured is an awareness of the extent to which the subjective frame of reference of the listener determines what is to be heard.[5]

If the counselor is not open to hearing theological meanings in the stories of persons who come for personal liberation, then he or she may only be adding to the person's barriers to freedom. For example, on one occasion I received some enlightening feedback from a man I had referred to a counselor for some sex therapy. The man said that the counselor had been able to deal well with all the emotions and experiences in life except one: when the client brought up a very meaningful and precious religious experience, it was ridiculed and labeled as neurotically defensive by the counselor. The client was crushed and angry over his vulnerable spiritual experience being mistreated by the counselor who could not hear genuine religious experience.

In another vein, Gerkin proposes that a theological frame of reference should determine the primary methodologies used in pastoral counseling:

> My theological concern for a depth understanding and response to the life of the soul will cause me to question the long-term depth implications of an emphasis upon pragmatic and forceful alteration of behavior. If the life of the soul does indeed involve the self's interpretive process within a framework of meaning that relates all aspects of life and relationships to a structure of ultimate meaning grounded in God, then the pastoral counselor as ministering carer of souls will wish to embrace in his or her work only those methodologies that hold forth the possibility of enlarging and enriching that interpretive process. Behavioral approaches to change will be seen as having real but limited usefulness in ministry seen as the care of souls.[6]

Listening to people and understanding the implicit theological meanings underlying human dynamics and interactions are both central to the purpose of pastoral counseling. By this means the counselor uncovers the client's operational theology

—the actual as opposed to professed belief system guiding his or her behavior. Such knowledge helps the counselor unravel the mystery of the client's world view. In this sense the pastoral counselor has a detective's unique vantage point in listening to, understanding, and intervening into the mysterious and distorted world of the client:

> In the classic murder mystery the sleuth is surrounded by a not-so-bright sidekick (the Watson figure) and not-so-bright police (the Lestrade figure). During the course of the story the police view the crime from a particular point of view which turns out to be false; they are continually led astray by following red herrings (clues which when followed too far lead an investigator in the wrong direction). The sidekick too is led astray by viewing events from the wrong perspective, although his comments sometimes help to illumine the problem for the sleuth. After a while, the sleuth solves the puzzle by considering the same "facts" the police and the sidekick did, but from a different perspective—usually "upside-down."[7]

What better person to understand the psychodynamics of persons from an upside-down perspective than the clinical theologian—the pastoral counselor. For the truth of the matter is that the upside-down perspective can often contain the right-side-up truth.

Idolatry as the Root of Pathology

The key listening perspective of operational theology is a hearing of a person's story in terms of what or who is perceived as the ultimate authority in the psyche of that person and of how he or she experiences being defined or valued by that ultimate authority. Self-concept always goes hand-in-hand with one's concept of ultimate authority; the doctrine of personhood is always related to the doctrine of God, whether one is avowedly religious or not. Thus the question of identity that is usually asked in our time—Who am I?—is not helpful outside of the relational question, Whose am I? Self is always defined in terms of Other or of a false "Other." Karl Jaspers is quoted as saying, "The kind of God image a human being has determines what kind of personality he is."[8]

The Christian philosophical position has been stated by J. V. Langmead Casserly: "In the history of human thought, the doctrine of God and the doctrine of man rise and fall together. The more profound our sense of the reality and meaning of divinity, the more vivid our apprehension of the unique status and dignity of human personality."[9] From the psychological point of view, Earl Loomis has stated this same truth: "Man's image of God and his image of himself are always linked together."[10] In other words, the self mirrors its own perceived absolute. A person is largely defined by what he or she places at the center and ground of his or her personality. The central focus of the inner world view is what tends to shape the personality of the individual. Jean Baker Miller and other secular therapists working at the Stone Center at Wellesley College use the phrase "the self-in-relation" to indicate that there is not a totally separate, isolated individuation process but rather there is always differentiation of self in relationship to another.[11]

Daim has posited that there is a personality center in the human being that is created for communion with the true ultimate.[12] Others, such as Thomas Merton, speak of this universal human need and striving for communion with God as being related to the *imago Dei*.[13] It is only when the center of the person's identity is linked to the eternal Thou or the ultimate Identity that one is truly oneself. Howard Thurman tells of an idea impressed upon him by his beloved grandmother, who had been a slave on a southern plantation: "The idea was given to her by a certain slave minister who, on occasion, held secret religious meetings with his fellow slaves. How everything in me quivered with the pulsing tremor of raw energy when, in her recital, she would come to the triumphant climax of the minister: 'You—you are not niggers. You—you are not slaves. You are God's children.' "[14] This black minister proclaimed the ultimate source of his people's identity. A fundamental task of pastoral counseling is to challenge idolatry: the worship of psychic false gods who usurp God's place at the center of the self and oppressively define people's identities.

Much popular psychology is concerned with helping people to overcome poor self-images and to develop better self-esteem. Such self-image psychology is usually based upon the assumption that people have misconceptions about themselves, correctable through a re-education process which may or may not include psychotherapy. Therapists invite people to challenge their debasing beliefs about themselves and to replace those misconceptions with more creative notions about themselves. But these professionals are often not aware that they are also confronting false concepts of ultimate authority in the persons with low self-esteem whom they are addressing. Thus the negative God-images and the lies flowing from those false ultimate authorities are being dealt with by professionals who are unaware that they are really dealing in clinical theology.

I believe that it is imperative for pastoral counselors to understand the idolatry that lies at the heart of most pathology. A person's erroneous view of self is interwoven with that person's erroneous view of God. Calvin Turley has said that the underlying cause of pathology is "a case of mistaken identity."[15] Essentially, persons are created in the image of God and only in being true to that inner self, linked with God, will emotional and spiritual well-being flow. When a person takes his or her identity from that which is less than the Ultimate Source of Being, then the sense of self is distorted. Various defenses and emotional and physical symptoms may appear over time which are covert modes of communicating that one is out of touch with one's true self and with the true God. Augustine was correct in saying, "Our hearts are restless until they rest in thee." Emotional and spiritual growth means moving more and more toward finding the heart and focus of one's personality linked with the true God as revealed in Jesus Christ.

A middle-aged client whom we shall call Eleanor is representative of persons who remain stuck with a mental representation of God which retards their emotional and spiritual development. Eleanor came to a pastoral counselor for help, complaining of ulcers and depression. She was a passive and submissive person who bottled up her feelings inside of herself. In the course of their conversations the pastoral counselor asked, "What do you think are some of the origins of your difficulty in sharing your feelings with others?" In reviewing clues to her emotional inhibitions, she remembered the conflicting messages she had received from her mother about hurt feelings. Her mother had read to her regularly from the Bible, particularly from her favorite scripture passage, the Beatitudes. Repeatedly, Eleanor's mother had read to her the words of Jesus, "Blessed are they that mourn: for they shall be comforted" (Matt. 5:4 KJV). This thought can be paraphrased with these words: "Blessed are they who can let themselves experience and express their hurts, disappointments, and grief, for they shall find healing and comfort." However, whenever her mother discovered that Eleanor was upset, sad, or tearful she would yell at her, "Shut up! Go to your room. Stop your crying. Don't be a crybaby."

The child heard two voices of authority in regard to dealing with experiences of hurt and sadness, the scolding mother and the scripture with the words of Jesus. Naturally, the mother's impact on Eleanor was greater when she was yelling than when she was reading from scripture. Thus, in dealing with hurt feelings Eleanor had followed the authority of the scolding mother rather than the spiritual authority of Jesus, and she felt guilty and bad if she experienced hurt feelings. The scriptural truth and biblical authority that affirmed the healing power of grieving was totally overwhelmed by the injunctions of the scolding mother. Eleanor learned early to stuff her feelings down inside of herself, which created the seedbed for ulcers and depression.

Eleanor had been faced with two contradictory teachings about grief issuing from two radically different authorities. Though both messages came to her from the lips of her mother, Eleanor had internalized the power of the scolding mother as the ultimate authority in dealing with her childhood pains, and that negative teaching about sadness had persisted into her adulthood. Eleanor learned too well that she could avoid criticism and anger if she repressed her sadness. Yet her very being protested the lie that her mother had taught her as gospel truth. Her body gave vent to the tensions of unexpressed emotions by developing ulcers. Her mind struggled with its imprisoned feelings through depression.

To make amends to the internalized, God-like scolding mother for her unacceptable feelings, Eleanor had in a sense crucified parts of herself through repression, depression, and psychosomatic illness. Eleanor's world view had put her critical mother-image in divine charge, and she had to distort her own mind and body in self-destructive ways in order to feel that she could survive in her hostile and alien world.

Fixation on an internalized parental image operating as a false ultimate authority in the human psyche leads to idolatry. Anna Freud and others have pointed out how children have a tendency to endow their parents and other significant authority figures with divine powers. The research of Rizzuto and McDargh has added powerful proof of the reality of the mental representations of God in the lives of everyone.[16] Daim states, "Empirical research of analytic processes confirmed that Freud was right in seeing the real root of neurosis in the fixation of the human being on an object of childhood. On closer examination we found that in every case the object of the fixation possesses an absolute character. The object of fixation in Freud's system is what we call an idol."[17] An idol is anything relative that is raised to an absolute, the finite elevated to the level of the infinite, or the transitory given the status of the permanent.

Pastoral counselors need to understand how developing mental representations of God play a significant role in either the emotional and spiritual growth or the arrested development of a person. This is a theological perspective on human development as well as on pathology. It is not to deny psychological, sociological, biological, and other viewpoints on understanding human nature. Rather, it is to assert that a theological listening perspective and a theological interpretation of what Anton Boisen called the living human documents is valid in both the understanding of and the counseling of persons.

The distorted world views, negative identifications of self, and erroneous belief systems of psychic idolatry are internalized scripts from childhood, and there is a strong tendency to replay those tapes throughout life. Howard Halpern has conceptualized the psychoanalytic repetition compulsion as "songs and dances":

> Inside our parents, as well as within us, there is an inner child, and this inner child frequently directs our parents' behavior just as it directs our own. Recorded in the brain cells of every person are the "videotapes" of every childhood experience and feeling, including fear, love, anger, joy, dependency, demandingness, insecurity, self-centeredness, inadequacy feelings, etc. . . . Also registered in our neurons are the commands, prejudices, injunctions and rules for living of our parents (and our parents' neurons contain the voices of their own parents). The combination of those tapes of all our early childhood feelings and reactions and the tapes of all the ways our parents behaved and all the injunctions and prescriptions for living they gave us compose what I have referred to as the inner child. Those stored transactions from our childhood can at times be "switched on" and replayed in the present as current feelings and behavior without being modified by a more grown-up experience, knowledge and wisdom. . . . I call the specific interactions that develop between the inner child in us and the inner child in our parents songs and dances because they have a repetitious, almost rhythmic, pattern. The same words, the same music, and the same dance are performed over and over.[18]

It is important to note that these "songs and dances" can lead to emotional and spiritual maturity. But our focus is on dealing with destructive world views, the self-sabotaging teachings and beliefs that get passed from generation to generation and catch people in idolatrous fixations. The pastoral counselor needs to listen to the life story, world views, beliefs, and gods of the counselee and then to present in appropriate therapeutic ways (sometimes unspoken) the story of the Christian revelation which the pastoral counselor embodies so that transformation may take place in the persons who come for help. Lies, masquerading as gospel truths, need to be confronted by authentic gospel truth.

Key Constructs

Operational Theology. Operational theology, in contrast to professed theology, looks beyond an individual's verbally and intellectually articulated theology to the dynamic images, mental representations of God, world view, maps of reality, belief systems, and value systems which actually dominate the life experience of people. Edwin A. Hoover defines operational theology as "a person's beliefs about the world, humankind and God, based on experience, perceptions, myths and hopes and that person's belief about his/her place in relation to all this."[19] Operational theology refers to the implicit religious story by which one is living, including unconscious material. Some persons use the term clinical theology as a synonym for operational theology.

Twin Idolatry or Double Idolatry. This concept refers to two related dimensions of psychic idolatry in which distorted and false perceptions of ultimate authority are directly linked with erroneous definitions and beliefs about one's self, one's identity and one's worth. The first aspect of idolatry deals with the mental representations of God explored in depth by Rizzuto. These false authority images, usually derived from experience with one or more parental or surrogate parental figures, are projected onto God. In Freud's day, the father image was usually the one projected onto God but today, in the United States, research indicates that the mother image is more frequently projected onto God.

This idolatrous view of ultimate reality is directly related to one's self-concept or self-image. The experience of a loving God, for example, fosters a more positive self-concept than that of a weak and impotent God who doesn't empower and affirm. And parents who affirm, validate, and confirm their children also give them a more positive mental representation of God than parents who are critical, judgmental, and blaming.

In order to survive in the symbolic world governed by a false ultimate authority, an individual has to construct a second idolatry around the self. This second idolatry is a reaction to the first idolatrous misperception of the nature of God. It can be thought of as a defensive strategy of salvation, or an attempt to provide one's own rescue in the face of a negative view of reality. The example of Eleanor dealing with her hurt feelings shows how in response to her scolding mother (whom she perceived as ultimate) she developed a defensive strategy of salvation, using repression, depression, and later on psychosomatic symptoms.

Some kind of "good works" offered to pacify the perceived god and to maintain a relationship with that authority may be part of the strategy of having to be one's own savior. A later chapter on self-justification will discuss just how, for the sake of survival in an idol-dominated world, the crucifixion of parts of the personality is accomplished. When there is no trust that the Loving Heart of Reality initiates atonement for humankind, then one has to find one's own survival strategies. Such self-atoning strategies range between the extremes of what Paul Tournier describes as the "neurosis of opposition" to the "neurosis of submission."[20] A person may seek to overthrow idolatrous, tyrannical forces by engaging in a plethora of acting out and rebellious behaviors. On the other hand, an individual may be an adaptive and submissive care-giver in order to pacify everyone and to feel safe in an insecure world. Recognizing the complexity of the possible patterns, our major focus is on the twin idolatries underlying the pathology of the client.

Tenacious Covenant in Idolatry. There is a binding covenant between the false god and the resulting false self. "You are my god and I am your person" is a statement of the impasse binding a false god to a false self. Daim posits that there is a personality center, or heart of the self, that yearns for communion with the ultimate. When a person is

31

not grounded in the Other, who is the true source of personhood, then the inner world is revolving around a false center. Walter Brueggemann says:

> The primary claim of "covenant"... is that human persons are grounded in Another who initiates personhood and who stays bound to persons in loyal ways for their well being. ... Covenant is the deep and pervasive affirmation that our lives in all aspects depend on our relatedness to this other One who retains initiative in our lives (sovereignty) and who wills more good for us than we do for ourselves.[21]

This intense attachment to the idol is related to the issue of resistance, to be explored later in some detail.

It should be noted that there may be areas of one's life in which one is free from the idol, even though many other segments of one's personality may be imprisoned in the idolatrous relationship. Daim believed that there is always a yearning for freedom and salvation from the idol.[22] Pastoral counseling seeks to connect with such yearnings in order to help people move beyond old idolatrous covenants into a new covenant. Using the language of object relations theory, the new covenant provides the holding environment in which persons can be mirrored, validated, and authenticated. In religious terminology, Thomas Merton speaks of the relational theology undergirding the new covenant with these words:

> Who am I? My deepest realization of who I am is—I am one loved by Christ. ... The depths of my identity is

the center of my being where I am known by God.[23]

We are fulfilled by an Identity that does not annihilate our own, which is ours, and yet is "received." It is a Person eternally other than ourselves who identifies Himself perfectly with ourselves. This Identity is Christ, God.[24]

In family therapy, covenants have been named "invisible loyalties"[25] by Boszormenyi-Nagy. They allow the false, limiting beliefs of the past which are passed down through the generations to become interpersonally validated convictions implanted during each person's childhood. A colleague tells of a case in which an idolatrous covenant with legalistic loyalties changed to a covenant of love and freedom. A young man, Harry, identified the bargain with his idol as "the game" in which there were specific rules. He identified the "rules of the game" as follows: "You have to be good and nice all of the time. You have to work hard every minute, or else you are not worthwhile. There is no place for joy in life, and if you start to seek it you better watch out because you will get completely off track and ruin your life. You are only worth loving when you are laden down with work and are acting nice and good. You will never succeed at being really loveable, but you'd better always keep trying, otherwise you are of no worth. I speak with the authority of the universe. This is how things are." Later in therapy, Harry was able to announce to his idol that the game was unsatisfactory. "The bargain I made with you is no longer satisfactory. I am not willing to play that way any more. Yet, I'm terrified of letting my persona shatter because I don't know how to relate any other way. I feel stuck between a rock and a hard place."[26]

Covenants are very strong, and people generally experience tremendous anguish in the process of trying to break free. Guilt feelings only make this more difficult. People usually have guilt feelings if they are not following the rules and teachings of an idol. For example, Eleanor felt guilty because her scolding mother taught her that expressing hurt feelings was bad. The real guilt concerning idolatry is generally not felt at all. In other words, not being connected to the true God or to the true self does not create any guilt. Tournier's discussion of true and false guilt is very helpful in this regard, though he did not connect it directly to the concept of idolatry.[27] Oftentimes the pastoral counselor needs to enable the person to see that the false guilt attracting so much of his or her attention clouds the fact that the person is caught in a covenant with an idol and needs to confess that idolatry.

Secular Scriptures. The teachings, values and beliefs transmitted by the idol are referred to as secular scriptures. These ideas operate in the human psyche as though they came down on tablets from Mount Sinai or were proclaimed by Jesus in the Sermon on the Mount. They carry divine weight for those caught in the idolatrous relationship. Secular scriptures are similar to what transactional analysis calls drivers, injunctions, and counter-injunctions; they are filled with shoulds, oughts, and musts. They usually include value statements about emotions, such as sadness and anger. For example, Eleanor was taught that her sad and hurt feelings were wrong and unacceptable. These teachings appear as sacred, revealed truths, but in reality they are destructive lies.

In pastoral counseling, I find that it is often helpful to bring to awareness the kinds of secular scriptures by which people are already living. The secular scriptures by which people are guiding their lives are already present, and it is a matter of bringing those teachings into awareness so that people may have more freedom to choose whether they want to continue to direct their lives by those destructive beliefs and values. Occasionally, it is helpful to contrast the secular scripture by which someone is living with a specially tailored quotation from scripture. For example, for a person whose fundamental secular scripture is, "I should be strong, nice, and giving, all of the time," I may misquote the Bible by saying, "Yes, blessed are the strong, for they shall inherit the world," or, "Unless you become as a strong parent you will not enter the kingdom of heaven." It is important to note that these secular scriptures have a powerful, tenacious nature, and they often can only be changed with great difficulty and struggle. However, when some people see that biblical authority and the spirit and teachings of Jesus are antithetical to their secular scriptures, they are sometimes more ready to give up their self-destructive thinking.

One woman in pastoral counseling identified her secular scriptures as her Decalogue. The laws for her life were: (1) Thou shalt not upset other people and hurt their feelings; (2) Thou shalt hold thyself back; (3) Thou shalt judge thyself harshly; (4) Thou shalt guide thyself by fear; (5) Thou shalt not let things come too easily; (6) Thou shalt not succeed for that would be sinful. In the transformations that took place in her therapy, she developed a "Revised Version" of her Decalogue: (1) I am alive and free; (2) I am soft, yielding, and open; (3) I am a vital and integrally important part of the flow of life; (4) I matter; (5) I am a spark of God which grows brighter and clearer every day; (6) I am flexible; (7) I am accepting and loving of all, especially of myself, a loveable human being; (8) I am honest, I am kind, I am patient; (9) I am abundant, filled with the presence of God; (10) I acknowledge I am familiar with fear; I can embrace it and confront it and step beyond; I am no longer guided by fear.

Understanding and making interventions in relation to secular scriptures may be a helpful part of the process of liberating persons from idolatry.

Secular Prayers. The dialogue implicitly going on between the self and the idol is called secular prayer. The process of communication between the idol and the self is a continuing one, even if the person is not aware of it. It is a reinforcing mechanism for the idolatrous covenant and involves a great deal of energy. Occasionally, it is helpful to articulate the implicit prayer the person is uttering to the false absolute. For example, it is not uncommon to find someone whose defensive strategy of salvation has been shattered by a crisis to be implicitly praying, "O God, please restore the same old secure, strong, and invulnerable patterns to me. I'm too scared of being vulnerable to life and open to its risks. Protect me from being fully human in this situation." I might suggest that this person consider choosing a different type of prayer, such as, "O God, please give me courage and openness in the midst of my fear and hurt that I may be empowered by you to grow by confronting this Jerusalem crisis of mine." Such corrective prayers cut to the heart of attempts at self-atonement. They often lead to a more trusting relationship with the Loving Heart of Reality.

Another person identified her implicit secular prayer in this way: "O God, give me this day all the comfort and security my parents provided me as a child many years ago. Keep me safe from evil as they defined it for me and as their parents defined it for them. Affirm my childhood belief that 'righteousness' and 'authority' (parents, teachers, preachers, politicians) are synonymous, and that it is not my lot to question but to obey. Free me from the pain of consequences which come from having made wrong decisions, and give me an authority I can trust to make decisions for me." Such secular prayers remind one of Thomas Oden's thought: "Life is the teacher who constantly instructs us on the vulnerability of our gods."[28]

The terrible power that the idol exerts over the captive, neurotic child-self has been set forth from an operational theology listening perspective. The task of pastoral counseling is truly taking on the gods, for as Fairbairn has said:

> I consider further that what is sought by the patient who enlists psychotherapeutic aid is not so much health as salvation from his past, from bondage to his "internal" bad objects, from the burden of guilt and from spiritual death. His search thus corresponds in detail to the religious quest.[29]

For various reasons, I shall limit my treatment of idolatry to neurotic problems. My purpose is to encourage theological thinking about clinical material and therapy, without going into the details of developmental psychology and psychodiagnosis from an object relations perspective. Also, I believe the world views of pastoral counselors tend to be somewhat neurotic in that they often feel overly responsible and indispensable.

M. Scott Peck, a psychiatrist, makes an interesting differentiation between a neurosis and a character disorder:

> Most people who come to see a psychiatrist are suffering from what is called either a neurosis or a character disorder. Put most simply, these two conditions are disorders of responsibility, and as such they are opposite styles of relating to the world and its problems. The neurotic assumes too much responsibility; the person with a character disorder not enough. When neurotics are in conflict with the world they automatically assume that they are at fault. When

those with character disorders are in conflict with the world they automatically assume that the world is at fault.[30]

While borderline clients are coming out of the woodwork in our clinical practices, I shall not be focusing on them. It is sufficient to note that adult borderline clients have not achieved a solid sense of evocative memory in the area of object relations, and therefore they struggle with a pervasive fear of abandonment by significant others. Their holding introjects, including their mental representation of God, tend to be functionally inadequate to keep separation anxiety in check. While theological constructs have some meaning for borderline and psychotic patients, it seems wise to limit the discussion of operational theology at this time to neurotic styles of living and the more garden variety types of problems that pastoral counselors confront.

It Is Easier to Ride a Camel in the Direction It Is Going

A desert father reportedly spoke centuries ago of the wisdom of joining people's resistance to change by saying, "It is easier to ride a camel in the direction it is going." Erroneous belief systems and fixated psychic idolatry often function like balky camels which resist going in any other direction besides that in which they are already headed. Learning to ride camels in a direction that they are already going is an important art and skill for the pastoral psychotherapist. Resistance can be understood as the individual's, couple's, or family's way of cooperating with therapy by acting out in the therapeutic context unresolved problems in their private lives which have been resistant to change. Even though some experts have recently spoken of the "death of resistance" and others have reframed resistant clients and systems as "misunderstood,"[1] I think it is more helpful to conceptualize resistance as occurring when idolatry and an erroneous belief system enter into interactions between the therapist and the client or client system.

Idolatrous world views and belief systems are often very persistent. People cling to their problems and their symptoms tenaciously. Though they have one hand extended outward for help, the other hand is often behind their backs holding tightly onto problematic situations. It is imperative that the pastoral counselor be aware that people who come for help often have a deep commitment to remaining just as they are. They often have an attachment to their difficult situation as it is, in spite of seeking counseling. People do not break their bondage to idolatry easily. Belief systems often seem embedded in cement. The repetition-compulsion, script, or life story that resists any changes says a great deal about the fixated operational theology of the counselee.

There is a popular story about a middle-aged man who went to a psychiatrist's office for an initial interview. After the man was seated, the doctor asked him what his problem seemed to be. The gentleman responded, "My problem is that I'm dead." The doctor asked, "You're dead?" "Yes, sir. My problem is I'm dead." The psychiatrist went ahead asking the usual questions for an intake session, but all he could get as a diagnosis from the patient was that the man considered himself to be dead. After wracking his brain, the psychiatrist said to the patient, "Sir, are there any particular things that would distinguish a dead person from a live one?" The patient pondered for a few moments and then replied, "Well, a dead person doesn't bleed when wounded and a live person does." "Ah ha," thought the psychiatrist to himself. He went to his desk and took out a sterile needle. Stealthily he plunged the needle into the arm of the patient sitting before him; blood spurted from the wound. The patient looked puzzled for a few moments, pondering the blood flowing from his arm. Then he looked up at the psychiatrist and said, "Son of a gun, Doc, dead men do bleed."

Individuals like this gentleman, plagued by negative and self-destructive experiences, have become so accustomed to their identity and ways of life that change is very frightening to them. Persons often develop an "at-homeness" with their perspectives and belief systems and find them difficult to give up. M. Scott Peck writes:

This process of active clinging to an outmoded view of reality is the basis for much mental illness. Psychotherapists refer to it as transference. Transference is that set of ways of perceiving and responding to the world which is developed in childhood and which is usually entirely appropriate to the childhood environment (indeed, often life-saving) but which is inappropriately transferred into the adult environment. . . . When problems of transference are involved, as they usually are, psychotherapy is, among other things, a process of map-revising. Patients come to therapy because their maps are clearly not working, but how they may cling to them and fight the process every step of the way! Frequently their need to cling to

their maps and their fight against losing them is so
great that therapy becomes impossible.[2]

What pastoral counselor has not anguished over
clients who have repeatedly made choices and
decisions that only reinforce negative and destructive treatment that the client experienced in
childhood?

This bringing of resistance to change into the
therapeutic environment is also true of couples and
families. In the alcoholic marriage one often sees
collusion between the alcoholic and the co-alcoholic
when the alcoholic goes on the wagon. The spouse,
who formerly may have cajoled and criticized the
problem drinker, may now buy the booze and try to
induce the mate to go back to drinking. The
co-alcoholic thus can continue to hide his or her
problems behind the partner's drinking. There is a
story about a gentleman who goes to a therapist and
asks for help for his wife, who thinks she is a hen.
After appropriate discussion and deliberation, the
counselor says, "I think that if you will bring your
wife to see me I may be able to help her." With
alarm, the client responds, "But I don't want to do
that because we need the eggs."

Family problems often very clearly represent
collusions in a family system that is resistant to
change. One paradigmatic family situation involves
an acting-out youngster who is the identified
patient in the family. The parents are distraught
over their child's behavior, and they put a lot of
energy in trying to get the child straightened out.

What a shock it can be to both the parents and the youngster when the therapist joins the resistance by saying to the youngster, "I want to commend you on your courage in trying to hold your parents' marriage together and in trying to keep them from looking at and dealing with their unresolved problems and conflicts. You are sacrificing a great deal of your life in order to focus their attention upon you and your seeming problems. There is an unspoken agreement in your family that you will protect your parents from their marital unhappiness and their individual personal problems."

Another example of a family demonstrating its resistance to change took place in the office of a well-known psychiatrist.[3] A couple and their ten-year-old son had been to numerous therapists, none of whom had been helpful to the family. At the end of the initial session with the new therapist, he gave homework to each of the parents to practice between sessions. The homework was based upon the observation, made during the initial hour, that the couple never spoke directly to each other but addressed each other through their son. The therapist said to the husband, "During the next week, when you want to say something to your wife I urge you to convey that message to her by directing the communication through your son." And to the wife the therapist communicated a similar message: "During the next week, when you want to share something with your husband, I encourage you to direct that communication

45

through your son to your husband." One week later the family returned, with the couple acting somewhat peeved with the therapist. They said, in effect, to the therapist, "If we want to talk to each other we'll talk directly to each other and we don't have to go through our son." So often in problematic families someone is caught in the middle and functions as the switchboard operator for the family's communications. Sometimes it is helpful in systems resistant to change to ride the camel in the direction in which it is already going.

Counselor Responses to Resistance to Change

The Exodus story provides a metaphor for the resistance to change. Escaping imprisonment in Pharaoh's Egypt may look appealing to us, but even with a Moses to lead the people to freedom some still yearned to quit the journey to the Promised Land when along the way they experienced the uncertainties of the wilderness. Some of them preferred to return to the familiar surroundings of Egypt than risk traveling further on the path to freedom.

Virginia Satir has said, "Resistance is mainly the fear of going somewhere you have not been."[4] Pastoral counselors who want to be helpful often have a difficult time affirming and validating the meaning and the reasons for their counselees' resistance to growing and changing. Neophyte pastoral counselors in particular often have a strong need to change clients in order to meet their own narcissistic needs for personal and professional success. The pastoral counselor can too readily come in on the "preacher wavelength" with an implicit or explicit message to the counselee that "You should be different; you ought to be different; you must be different."

Counselors who stubbornly press for people to change without appreciating and understanding their resistance may need to explore their own countertransference issues, and why they are applying such pressure for change. For example, does the counselor have an internal, perfectionistic demand that she or he *has* to be successful and helpful in counseling? Sometimes a counselor needs to consider whether he or she is functioning in such demanding ways because of a fear of failure. If pastoral counselors have some unresolved issues from their childhoods, then they may be attempting unconsciously to get the client to change as they were not successful in getting the members of their own families to change.

In any event, a counseling stance that demands a change in the counselee usually only creates more resistance and defensiveness in the person seeking help. In such instances, the counselor may need to side with the resistance rather than against the resistance. A story that perfectly illustrates this idea for me is attributed to one of the pioneers in paradoxical therapy. When he was a youngster living on the farm, he noticed his father one day trying to get a balky calf into the barn. The harder the father pulled on the calf to get her into the barn, the more stubborn she seemed to become. After watching the frustration of his father and the resistance of the calf, the lad burst his sides laughing at his father's predicament. In frustration his father finally said to him, "Well, if you think you can do any better, then you come over here and get this cow into the barn." With a sudden flash of insight, the boy dashed over to the rear of the animal, pulled her tail in the direction away from the barn, and the calf moved forward directly into the barn.[5]

If one can help a balky cow or a client move ahead in a direct, rational way, then obviously one seeks to go in that direction. However, when the resistance does not seem amenable to rational or logical approaches, then one may try other maneuvers involving the use of paradoxical thinking. For centuries, parents have used reverse psychology with children, particularly in instances in which the parent felt the child was stubbornly trying to manipulate the parent. The child who tries to manipulate the parent by threatening to run away may discover that the strategy is rendered ineffective by the parent suggesting that he or she help the child to pack a suitcase.

On occasions when the rational and the logical do not seem to be effective, it may be more important to relate to people from the nonrational side. Allen Fay writes:

> Many people can be persuaded to give up mistaken beliefs by presenting facts, evidence, data, and logical arguments, but a fixed, irrational belief is usually not amenable to persuasion or logic. . . Rationality frequently does not effectively combat irrationality,

whereas even greater irrationality does. Seeing our irrationality in someone else especially in an exaggerated form, tends to force us to take a stand against it. We are not likely to recognize irrationality in ourselves until it is mirrored to us by someone else.[6]

Addressing the nonrational beliefs and behaviors of counselees through nonrational interventions such as paradoxical thinking can be understood as a kind of consciousness-raising—a bringing into awareness of self-defeating beliefs and patterns which are harmful and destructive to the life of an individual, couple, or family. In a strange way, a paradoxical intervention is like a Rogerian reflection stating the essence of the client's nonrational communication. Using such paradoxical thinking is a way of stating the beliefs and decisions by which people are already living and which they persist in using to direct their lives.

Another way of viewing paradoxical interventions is as an attempt to help the client to confess his or her true belief system. Such a confession of one's operative belief system can lead to the possibility of repentance, the freedom to choose another direction, or a turning to new patterns of living and coping with life. In any event, unless the nonrational beliefs are acknowledged or confessed it is highly unlikely that repentance, change, and a metanoia can take place in the person, the couple, or the family. An awareness, an acknowledgment, or a confession of the idolatrous world view and belief system in which one is fixated may help one gain the freedom to make a new choice in life. The pastoral counselor can be an enabler or catalyst in helping people to decide whether they want to continue to live according to their usual world view, beliefs, and values or whether they wish to choose other beliefs and values by which to live.

The pastoral psychotherapist often has to help people see the ruts in which they have been functioning, in the hope that they may have some freedom to choose other patterns. There is a story from Maine about a sign standing at the juncture of a paved road and a dirt road. Those familiar with spring thaws in cold climates know that it is common for car and truck tires to make deep ruts in the mud of those roads during thaws, which then solidify in place when freezing temperatures return. In recognition of those potential frozen ruts, the signpost read, "Choose your ruts wisely; you'll be in them for the next nine miles." People's erroneous world views, self-sabotaging belief systems, and defensive strategies of salvation dictated by their idolatrous scripts are like those ruts in which one is so readily stuck.

Pastoral counselors need to understand the bottom line of people's resistance to change. People have good subjective reasons, which they often deny even to themselves, for the stuck places in their psyches which are so resistant to change. Usually, there are safety and security needs embedded in those good subjective reasons that make it next to impossible for the person to change. Even though the reasons may not make sense to the counselor at first, it is imperative that they be made clear. Often it is only when one can see the payoffs and rewards of apparently self-defeating behavior that one may become free to make other choices.

Harold Greenwald, in his work on direct decision therapy, has said:

> It has dawned on me that almost all successful therapy, no matter what the orientation, ends up with the same result; the patient makes a decision to change. Usually it is a decision to change his life choice, or if you prefer, life style, or his way of being in the world. . . . It also seemed to me that the character which the patient presents was the result of a whole series of previous decisions. This does not mean that I deny or refuse to acknowledge the existence of other factors. Of course there is his biological inheritance and the influence of his total life history. But still there is room for him to decide how to employ what he has inherited and what he has learned. It is in this area of choice that psychotherapy asserts its major influence.
>
> Having come to this conclusion I started to work out a method which I . . . could best employ to work directly to produce the decision to change. Now I see it as a three-step process: (1) To find out by what decisions the person is now operating. (2) To have him recognize that his present way of life is the result of previous choices and therefore he probably can, if he so chooses, make a different choice and help him see the variety of such choices; in other words, the options open to him. (3) To help him carry through the new choice and to study with him what hang-ups are in the way of having him implement his new choice.[7]

Let us look at a few examples of how people's good subjective reasons, often denied even to themselves, keep them operating in fixed ways. Take, for example, the story of a nonorgasmic woman. In trying to understand over time the good subjective reasons why it was important for her to be nonorgasmic with her husband, she became aware of a number of childhood experiences that made it next to impossible for her to be orgasmic. A major reason was her fear of losing control. Not allowing herself to move spontaneously in the sexual encounter with her husband was a way of protecting her identity and of not losing the integrity of her individuality. By helping her to become aware of, to acknowledge, and to confess those good subjective reasons why it was important for her to be nonorgasmic, she was left with more freedom to decide whether she wanted to remain in that same pattern. Affirming the client's good subjective reasons and his or her freedom to choose even self-sabotaging patterns out of fear or insecurity is a significant therapeutic stance in the riding of a camel in the direction in which it is going.

In another example, a married man who was involved in an affair was confronted by his wife with his extramarital relationship. She told him that he had one month to make a decision to either give up his mistress or to lose his marriage. He struggled in anguish and shared with his therapist the sleeplessness, the headaches, and the general physical malaise that he was experiencing. His therapist suggested that while his physical symptoms were problematic, the client secretly preferred to express his anxiety physically rather than confront such uncomfortable feelings. The therapist suggested that, in fact, the client was like a donkey looking at one bale of hay to his left and another bale to his right and afraid of moving toward either one for fear that he would lose the other. Deciding not to decide, with all of its attendant disadvantages, may at the same time have the advantage of providing some safety protection from loss and risk.

Sometimes it is very difficult for counselors who want to see their clients change to genuinely affirm the rights of clients to choose not to change. The pastoral counselor sometimes may need to be guided by the awareness of how God goes on loving each of us even though we are not obedient or being responsive to what would be the best for us, or in accordance with the will of God. In affirming the resistance of clients to change, the pastoral counselor needs to incorporate paradoxical thinking into his or her own natural style. (However, one ought not to utilize a technique in dealing with resistance that is not compatible with one's own personality and value system.) It is also important not to use paradoxical thinking with the spirit of sarcasm or with a critical attitude. It is relatively easy to use paradoxical thinking as a put-down, which can readily undermine the therapeutic relationship.

Pastoral counselors also need to be flexible and prescriptive in terms of the persons with whom they use paradoxical thinking. Some counselees find paradoxical interventions emotionally repugnant, and they react defensively to them. Thus, while paradoxical interventions seek to free people from their resistance, they can also escalate defensiveness and resistance. Having a philosophical, unhostile sense of humor in utilizing paradox with counselees can be a helpful stance in this instance.

While some pastoral counselors may not identify resistance per se, many can acknowledge that resistance is "alive and well and living under an assumed name."[8] For example, those who have a behaviorist orientation may speak in terms of compliance and noncompliance. Some people in family therapy may view resistance as the family's unique way of cooperating in the therapy by reliving in the therapeutic relationship repetitive family problems.

Typical Case

Let us look at a common type of case depicting a neurotic situation. In the person's history, the parental figures have not been dependable authority figures. In terms of emotional advocacy for the client, they have been either critical and judgmental or distant and absent. The client developed a reaction formation in the process of growing up so that the child was a parent to the parents, and has continued that role in the adult world, being superwoman or superman in marital, family, and professional relationships. The twin idolatry is of an adversarial God whom one has to try to appease by being superachieving and super-good.

In the therapeutic process there is often great resistance to moving into a person's vulnerable, trusting little child self, where there can be genuine spontaneity and open communication of one's needs and feelings. The pastoral counselor has a number of options in dealing with resistance through joining the world view and belief system of the client. One approach is to empathically share with the client that it is very important for the client not to risk getting close to his or her child self or to God. By depending upon God one will become vulnerable to another role reversal, in which the person will end up taking care of God just as one has taken care of other supposed authority figures from childhood. In other words, the good subjective reasons for staying in the super-person role are that one is more in control and less vulnerable to the possibilities of disappointment, hurt, and being controlled by others.

One could also intervene with a secular scripture statement such as "Blessed are the supermen and superwomen for they shall inherit the world." Or one could, again, use the distorted scripture, "Unless you become as a strong parent you will not enter the Kingdom of Heaven." On another level, one might intervene with the secular prayer that the implicit theme of the client in communication with the counselor as well as with God is "Please help me to pull these pieces together so that I can be strong once again and be in control. Forbid that I should be vulnerable, weak, and need to have others take care of me."

With some theologically oriented clients it is possible to talk very directly about the twin idolatry that is going on. One can discuss the projection of the authority image from a parental figure onto the Godhead and the resulting defensive strategy of salvation in which one's sense of mistaken identity leads one to crucify and distort the personality in order to survive in the world ruled by the idol. Occasionally, one may also try to help the client to see that the survival strategy adopted during childhood and persisting into adulthood is the very thing presently blocking the person's openness to a more mature level of living and of being truly able to receive love and the gift of salvation. Sometimes a person may experience a kind of emotional and spiritual nausea in looking at his or her lack of courage and faith to challenge the decisions made in early childhood. However, that very disgust and the potential resulting aggression against the idol may result in transformation.

In some way, communicating caring and love for people mistakenly riding their emotional and spiritual camels *away* from salvation may be the very thing that opens them to the possibility of grace. For example, a counselee who was going through a narcissistic and defensive withdrawal during a painful experience was deeply touched when his counselor told him that he would accompany the client on his inward journey of detachment and withdrawal. As Christ descended into hell, so the pastoral counselor, descending into the intrapsychic and interpersonal hells of clients, may be a witness to the truth that God's redemptive and healing love is present even though a person has "made his bed in Sheol."

A Theological Perspective

From a theological perspective, resistance is persistence in idolatry. Resistance at its root is the tenacious holding on to one's erroneous world view; to one's fundamental misconception of ultimate reality and one's place and identity within that reality; and to one's misperception of the nature of God, the nature of humans, and the ultimate meaning of life. It is the persistent belief that one's own story of life is the true perspective and that the revelation of the story of the gospel of the good news is not true for oneself. Resistance fundamentally blocks revelation, grace, gospel, and good news. It means choosing one's own defensive strategy of salvation in a frightening world and turning away the gift of salvation from the gracious, loving God focused in the personhood of Jesus Christ. Under its influence, one chooses to crucify oneself by crippling one's personality in various ways instead of receiving the forgiving and empowering love of God in the crucified and risen Christ.

Resistance means that one persists in the idolatrous view of an ugly or absent God to whom one has to make one's own atonement rather than trusting in the amazing, initiatory love of God who made the only atonement necessary. It has elements of narcissistic defiance and despair, communicating "I'd rather do it myself" than be open to the possibilities of grace. Resistance seeks to minimize risks by encapsulating anxiety, thus guarding safety and security. Mandating a distrusting stance as compared to a faithful openness, resistance is a turning in on oneself, toward womblike security, because the world is not to be trusted. Finally, resistance is choosing the isolation of personal hell because one is so afraid of the risk of love.

In the face of resistance, the pastoral counselor is the embodiment and mediator of the possibilities for becoming a new creature in Christ. Loving and caring for another who strongly resists this new creation by clinging to the old world views, mistaken belief systems, and self-defeating idolatries is a part of the inward cross that the counselor carries for redemptive and healing purposes.

The Implicit Religious Drama in Marital and Family Counseling

The Impact of Idolatry on One's Marital Choice and Interactions

During a meeting of a women's therapy group that was discussing sex, Claudia shared her story with embarrassment but also with courage. "My husband, Bruce, never wants to have sex relations with me, and I feel like some kind of nut because I'm so frustrated. It seems strange to me that most of the women I talk to about intimate things complain because their husbands want too much sex. But that is not true of my marriage. My husband never wants to go to bed with me. That shatters me. What is wrong with me as a woman? Am I not enough of a woman, so that he does not desire me? Or am I such an oversexed woman that I cannot accept what Bruce says are the normal sexual patterns of married life? Sometimes I am afraid that I am abnormal or perverted because of my sexual desires. My mother made me feel that sex was dirty and sinful. She said that men were animals and that a woman had to put up with sex as a marital duty. But my doctor has told me that mother's attitude was not right. A woman has a right to expect sexual fulfillment in marriage. He says that I am not abnormal because I want to have sex relations and to enjoy them. He has even suggested a number of times that I have some affairs so that I can find sexual fulfillment that way. I wonder what you all think about that suggestion. I must admit that at times I am tempted to follow the doctor's advice just to see if I could really be happy in a sexual relationship and perhaps even to show that husband of mine that I could get along without him. But I'm afraid that I'd feel so guilty that I'd be in a worse mess if I had an affair."

During this discussion, one of the group members asked, "Did you have any clues prior to your marriage that your husband would be like this?" Claudia replied, "Yes, I realize now that there were some indications of this back before we got married, but I didn't see it that way then. I remember how I had a number of fellows who dated me, and they all tried to go as far as they could in making out with me. But my upbringing caused me to dislike aggressive men and to think that those who tried to make out were really sinful and dirty and didn't really care about me. They only wanted sex. Then along came Bruce and he was so different from all the rest. He was so nice and gentlemanly. He didn't try to make me; in fact, it was only after many months of dating that he even kissed me goodnight. I felt that he respected me and that he was a person of high moral and spiritual character. So I married him. Now I know that I misread his 'virtue.' I thought that it was all noble and good, but now I can see that much of it was fear, inhibitions, and sexual problems."

A number of moral and ethical questions are involved in Claudia's story. Of course, a major issue is the tragic advice that having an affair will resolve her marital and sexual problems. The question of healthy attitudes toward sex is another moral concern, as is whether she should stay with her husband. But important as these problems are, let us focus on a theological implication too often overlooked in marriage counseling situations. Let us try to relate the concept of idolatry and false belief systems to mate selection and marital interaction.

From the material presented above and from other evidence, it was clear that in her youth Claudia had accepted her mother as her ultimate authority on attitudes toward sex. She had internalized her mother's values as she perceived them, so that all aggressive men seemed bad and passive men like Bruce, good. (In all fairness, it is important to point out that the child's image of the parent may be somewhat different from the real parent. Claudia's mother may not have been as prudish, puritanical, and moralistic as Claudia thought, but nonetheless she acted according to her *perceived* image of her mother. As Eric Berne wrote: "One acts and feels, not according to what things are like, but according to one's mental image of what they are like."[1]) Claudia had the idolatrous belief that her mother was the good and true ultimate authority and that her advice regarding boy-girl relationships, sex, and marriage was the gospel truth. As this case illustrates, the idol creating a disruptive influence in a person's life has usually to some extent been perceived as good. The idol's authority has not been questioned, and one identifies the idol's attitudes and teachings as good and one's own needs and feelings as bad.

The effects of the idolatry of parental images in marriage are also depicted in a cartoon showing a newly married couple timidly lying next to each other in bed. Hanging on the wall above the bed are portraits of their parents scowling down judgmentally at the couple. The frowning parental faces seem to say: "You are a bad boy and a bad girl for wanting to indulge in sexual relations." The observer can see the shame and guilt emanating from the faces of the lovers.

Let us look at another case highlighting the role of idolatry in marriage. In an initial interview with Jane, I was startled to hear her abrubtly announce: "Men are no damn good; this is my third alcoholic husband." However, she also worried that there was something wrong with her, given her repeated choice of such men. "I want to know why these most important relationships keep going haywire," she implored.

As she reviewed her life, Jane realized that she had been taking care of emotional cripples since early childhood. Her mother had been a fragile woman who would cry, get a headache, and/or take to her bed at the drop of an emotional feather. Since the age of four, Jane had been responsible for her mother's feelings, and she had tried to protect her mother from any pressures, criticisms, or hurts. Jane decided that it was not safe to entrust her mother with her own child-self, so she exchanged being a daughter for being her mother's mother.

Jane's father was a volatile man, and she quickly learned to pacify him so that nothing in the household environment could kindle his fury. She sought to protect both herself and her mother from her father's emotional immaturity and explosiveness. Jane was a child of "four going on forty," deprived of an environment that had reliable authority figures to whom she could entrust her child-self. When it came to her selection of a mate, she simply continued her childhood pattern of protecting and parenting immature persons.

During courtship, a person may be aware of but ignore subtle clues that certain characteristics in the future mate's personality revive the unresolved conflicts and patterns of childhood. One may also idealize potential mates as the opposite of early significant others, denying that the other has qualities similar to those of the idolatrous authorities of youth. In fact, the beloved may even be seen as a romantic savior figure who will deliver one from all the deprivations and hurts of the past.

Later, in the process of interacting together in marriage, the couple may find that idealized images fade and more negative images are aroused. A reactivation of the unresolved conflict with the idol image may then develop, to be unconsciously acted out in the spousal relationship. The partner then receives the projection of the bad parental image, and the complex feelings associated with the idol are directed at him or her. Thus the basic problem of unresolved idolatry originating in the child-parent relationship is reenacted in the marital relationship. While a person may say in anger to a spouse, "Oh, you're just like my father (or mother)," she or he does not realize that she or he has built into the marriage relationship the unresolved idolatrous relationship with the internalized father or mother. The pastoral counselor needs to be aware that the "holy deadlock" of certain marriages may be the result of the re-creation of unresolved childhood idolatries within the marriage.

In fact, the pastoral counselor can hypothesize that marital reenactment of idolatrous relationships is an attempt to resolve the idolatries, similar to the way one tries to master unresolved traumas through repetitive dreams. Unfortunately, couples caught up in the web of such conflicts are usually unable to see their struggle as an opportunity to resolve the underlying problem of idolatries even as they work to improve their relationship. Thus counseling can help these unhappy couples to understand how the harmful messages and deceptive lies of their intrapsychic idols have destroyed marital harmony just as they robbed them of personal peace.

Leave Before You Cleave

If one believes that the unresolved "songs and dances" of childhood lead to marital conflict, then one also must believe that premarital counseling involves intensive work with a couple's family histories. Premarital counseling and education as well as growth experiences for the newly wed may encourage people to look at family patterns, beliefs, and values, which can be either building blocks for or potential barriers to marital growth. Couples can learn how they bring the different patterns, rules, roles, and expectations of their childhood histories into a new relationship. A colleague told the story of an argument between himself and his wife early in their marriage which illustrates how conflicts grow out of different histories. One Sunday, as he poured the gravy prepared by his wife onto his meat and potatoes, he queried, "What's wrong with this gravy? It's much too thick." She immediately countered, "There's nothing wrong with the gravy. It's perfectly good gravy." During the ensuing argument, the couple figured out the nature of the problem: his mother always made thin gravy and to him good gravy was *thin* gravy, but her mother always made thick gravy and to her *thick* gravy was good gravy. The tension was immediately broken when they reached this understanding. Simply accepting historical differences instead of making negative judgments about them is a mature step in the development of relationships.

If I were to offer any warranty for premarital

counseling guaranteeing the stability of a marriage for some years, I would back it up by meeting separately with each partner and with their extended family networks. Even though few couples or their extended families are presently open to such a conversation with a pastoral counselor, I think premarital counseling involving the families of potential marriage partners is on the horizon and could include the following process. After discussion with the couple alone, the pastoral counselor asks each of them to invite the significant others from their childhoods for at least a two-hour meeting. One meeting is held with the intended groom and his family, and a separate meeting is held with the intended bride and her family. The focus for discussion is the family history and the relationships and events which have helped to form the personality of the person to be married. The "songs and dances" of the past are discussed while the family reminisces about such key events in the individual's life as birth, health, early years, beginning school, puberty, adolescence, et cetera. The rules and patterns of family life are also reviewed. Family photo albums and the like may also help to facilitate the discussion. A goal is to help the individual be more aware of the history one brings to a marriage so one can be freer to choose how to function in the new, married life.[2] People need to be liberated from the "household gods" of the past so they can be free to choose their own God and to become responsible and accountable for their own lives and marriages.

Two Metaphors for Intimate Relationships and Communication

While growing up every child has two fundamental needs, which have been given various
names, including the terms roots and wings. *Roots*
refers to the human need for affiliation, belonging,
togetherness, community, and communion. *Wings*
refers to the need for differentiation, freedom, and
individuation. Developmental psychologists have
posited these two fundamental human personality
needs: to be in relationship with significant others
and to evolve one's own unique identity. Pathology
often develops when a child's or youth's family fails
to fulfill these fundamental needs. A youngster
should not have to choose between love or freedom,
acceptance or individuality. Each person needs
both. In discussing the childhood of Jesus, Paul
Tournier notes that Jesus did not have to choose
either "the neurosis of submission" or "the neurosis
of opposition."[3] The following two stories exem-
plify relationship patterns that either restrict and
inhibit one's freedom to be or facilitate and
empower one to be.

The first story is about the middle-aged gentleman who went into a bargain-basement clothing
store to purchase a suit. After trying on one of the
suits, he was looking at it in the mirror when a clerk
approached. The customer said to the clerk, "The
sleeves are too long on the jacket." "Well then,
hunch over your shoulders so the sleeves will be
pulled up, and then the sleeves will fit all right,"

said the clerk. The gentleman hunched his shoulders over and, sure enough, the sleeves came up to a position where they appeared to fit. "Well, the pant legs are also too long," said the customer. "Well, then, crouch down and bend your knees somewhat and that will help to lift the pant legs to the right length," said the clerk. The customer obliged and found that the pants now fit as he stood somewhat crouched and hunched over. The gentleman said, "Well, I guess I'll purchase the suit and wear it home." On his way out of the store, wearing his new suit and walking hunched over so that the suit would fit, he encountered two women coming into the store. One woman whispered to the other, "Look at that poor deformed gentleman." "Yes," said the other, "but isn't that a nice fitting suit."

That story encompasses too much of what has passed for sound and even Christian child rearing practices. Too often, authorities force others into psychological and spiritual ill-fitting suits that may be of a pleasing appearance to others but are destructive to the authentic nature of the adaptive person. Too often in intimate relationships one pays the price of sacrificing the true self in order to fit in with the expectations of others and to gain their approval and acceptance. But this is a violation of the true self, of the image of God in oneself. For the sake of survival one dresses in the false self—a crippling condition but one allowing oneself to get along with others.

The second story is about a ten-year-old boy who went with his mother and fifteen-year-old sister to a restaurant for lunch one day. After the waitress had taken the mother's and the sister's orders, she turned to the boy and said, "And young man, what will you have?" The mother interrupted, "I'll order for him." The waitress overlooked the comment of the mother and turned again to the boy and said, "And young man, what will you have?" This time the teenage sister interrupted and said, "I'll order for him." The waitress remained patient and looked again at the boy. "And young man, what will you have?" The boy replied, "A hamburger." The waitress asked, "How would you like it? Rare, medium, or well-done?" The boy responded, "Well-done." The waitress continued, "What would you like on your hamburger? Catsup, relish, mustard, or pickles?" The boy reflected a moment and then responded, "Catsup, relish, mustard, and pickles." The waitress turned from the table, and headed for the kitchen, saying, "One hamburger, well-done, with the whole works, coming up." The boy turned to his mother and said, "Gee, Mom, she thinks I'm real."

This story reflects the fundamental human yearning to be validated, mirrored, confirmed, and authenticated. Maurice Freedman has noted that "if confirmation is central to human and inter-human existence, then it follows that disconfirmation, especially in the earlier stages of life, must be a major factor in psychopathology, or what is properly miscalled 'mental illness.' "[4] Carl Rogers speaks of the essence of such validation this way: "When I am not prized and appreciated, I not only feel very much diminished, but my behavior is actually affected by my feelings. When I am prized, I blossom and expand, I am an interesting individual. In a hostile or unappreciative group, I am just not much of anything. . . . Thus, prizing or loving and being prized or loved is experienced as very growth enhancing. A person who is loved appreciatively, not possessively, blooms and develops his own unique self."[5]

Theologically, one might say that God created the children of the earth to be loved and confirmed in all their uniqueness and realness. The nature of God's love is to affirm each person's unique identity and to provide a holding, caring environment for each, that each might blossom in his or her own special way. The therapeutic process is in many ways a corrective to faulty child-rearing practices, with the counselor mediating more of the nature of the divine parent who can love the individual into her or his true and authentic self. The false self and neurotic adaptations can then be surrendered, because self-destructive personality sacrifice is not required by the Eternal Heart.

Idols tend to clothe persons in ill-fitting suits. But God does not impose an agenda onto another's life, but lovingly invites and calls forth the unique agenda within the heart of each person. The worship of idols leads to the formation of a false self; the love of God invites the true self into abundant life.

The Impact of Idolatry Upon Communication

Many authorities agree that the key to developing intimacy is creative communication. Constructive communication is a cornerstone for building healthy, intimate marital and family relationships. The belief and value systems concerning patterns of communication are often inextricably bound up with false gods. From a theological listening perspective, it can be helpful to try to understand the injunctions and directives of the household gods in regard to the communication of feelings and needs within the family system.

The messages about communication—both overt and covert—from the authorities within a family system can be crucial in determining whether an individual is emotionally bound by an ill-fitting suit of rules about sharing and communicating or whether he or she is confirmed as real in the spontaneous expression of feelings and needs. Idols have their ways of teaching such secular scriptures as "Don't feel, don't be, don't have needs; all your needs and feelings are selfish," and "Sacrifice your needs and feelings in order to take care of the rest of us." Again and again we find persons who decided in the process of growing up that their survival depended on never expressing any needs or sharing certain feelings in the family context. Even so-called Christian judgments are utilized to declare the healthy, spontaneous expression of needs and feelings to be selfish, sinful, evil, and un-Christian.

How much emotional and spiritual havoc has been wreaked by authority figures who have communicated to others that thinking your own thoughts, having your own feelings, and articulating your own needs are destructive (if not demonic) acts? What an upside-down world, where people are taught that being in touch with their humanness and sharing it with significant others is un-Christian, bad, or unhealthy behavior. Most pastoral counselors can think of numerous persons with whom they have counseled who have suffered from an idol's misnaming of normal, natural, and God-given needs and feelings as bad, sinful, and demonic. It is incredible to meet people who have been self-sacrificing, generous to a masochistic fault, and submissive to others, who, because of mislabeling and critical judgments from authorities, believe themselves even in adulthood to be selfish because they experience these fundamental human needs.

Let us explore a few key emotions that are often given negative value judgments by false authority figures, thus constricting one's ability to develop intimacy and a sense of freedom in family relationships. An idol can place value judgments on whether it is all right to have these emotions as well as to express them.

Sexual feelings, fantasies, and needs are often a locus for negative judgments by the false absolutes. Some experts say that religion has been more destructive to mental health in this area of life than in any other because the religious stance has tended to communicate value judgments of bad news about sexuality rather than communicating the good news about the responsible and creative use of sexuality in the context of God's creation. This painful struggle over one's sexuality can be illustrated in thousands of ways. The poignant story of a woman who had been married for more than twenty years who could not go to church to worship God on Sunday morning if she had had intercourse with her husband on Saturday night reflects the terrible dichotomy of the good, religious person and her bad and disapproved sexuality. Sometimes rebellion against the condemning and restrictive sexual authority leads people to the destructive and debilitating experience of sexual permissiveness masquerading as sexual freedom. In myriad examples of sexual conflicts and pain, the underlying sexual value systems which have been a part of the secular scriptures from idolatrous figures have caused untold psychic harm to millions of people.

Idols also often communicate destructive messages and false beliefs about anger and its appropriate expressions. On the one hand, many erroneous religious beliefs, such as "it is un-Christian to be angry," lead to the repression of anger. The bottling up of frustrations and emotional hurts leading to anger has caused all kinds of negative reaction in the human psyche as well as the somatization of anger into various illnesses. On the other side of this belief is the equally dangerous assumption that the unbridled verbal and physical expression of anger is justifiable. Cognitive therapists have helped us to understand that while the ventilation and catharsis modes of expressing anger can be helpful in some instances, there are also anger-creating philosophies permitting people to make arrogant, absolutist demands on others and to remain fixed in their anger until the other person gives in. Each person needs to discover for him or herself the various verbal, physical, and written ways in which anger can be expressed helpfully and therapeutically, both for oneself and for others. Beyond the appropriate ventilation and expression of anger, one should also be aware of the poisonous effects of arrogantly demanding that others behave exactly according to one's prescribed expectations. Changing internal assumptions and beliefs about how other people must be or should be can be a primary step toward freedom from chronic anger.

The emotional experience and expression of fear, inadequacy, insecurity, and helplessness have also often been taboo. Oftentimes the false authorities have communicated that a person should not have those kinds of feelings, or at least not disclose fear and insecurity to others. Men in particular have been taught that it is unmasculine to reveal these feelings. People may act like the Rock of Gibraltar on the outside when they really are frightened and alone on the inside. People often communicate anxieties and insecurities as anger and blame. I recall having heard an adult woman relive a childhood experience of having fallen out the window of a moving car. When her father stopped the car and ran back to check on his little girl, he yelled at her for falling out of the car. She had no sense that her father was worried and afraid for her safety, and that he was masking it behind a facade of anger and blame. It is a sad experience when, in growing up, one only connects with the strong, defensive side of a parent and not with his or her insecurities and helplessness.

This defensive protection against revealing one's inadequacies is reminiscent of the preacher who wrote himself a note in the margin of his sermon manuscript which read, "Weak point. Pound pulpit harder." Or take the situation of a middle-aged husband who is afraid of losing his virility. He has had the embarrassing experience of not being able to follow through to completion an act of lovemaking with his wife. Too humiliated to talk openly with his wife, he may seek to bolster his sagging ego by having an affair. If he were able to share his feelings with his wife in words such as, "Dear, I am afraid that I am really slowing down and I'm not the man I once was," he might be pleasantly surprised to hear his wife's responding, "Don't worry about that. You've been a sexual athlete all these years, and it's good to have you slowing down. Besides, there are so many other important aspects to our marriage now." Helping people to gather the courage and the faith to identify and to share their fears and insecurities is another dimension of breaking through faulty belief systems dictated by idolatrous authorities.

If I had an opportunity to help people to transform just one erroneous, idol-derived value judgment regarding the expression of emotions in the intimacy of family life, I would choose to help people to identify and express hurt, disappointment, loss, and grief. One of the major ways that family therapy helps to liberate people is in exposing what appears, on the surface, to be negative, rebellious behavior as expressions of emotional pain and hurt. Reframing defensive reactions of sulking, acting out, and destructive anger as stemming from hurt and emotional pain can be a major step in helping marital and family relationships to grow. The truth of Jesus' statement, "Blessed are they that mourn, for they shall be comforted," needs to carry corrective authority to challenge an erroneous belief system that tends to frustrate, inhibit, and block the healthy emotional expression of hurt and pain.

It is incredible to behold the variety of harmful belief systems concerning the sharing of love, caring, warmth, affection, and tenderness in the context of the family, which was *created* for the giving and receiving of love. How often people are taught, implicitly or explicitly, that it is not safe to show love, and, in fact, that if one gets close to another, one is setting oneself up for being hurt. If we have been hurt too much in close relationships we may try to keep ourselves safe from the involvements of loving and the possibility of being hurt again.

Yet having the courage to care and to reach out to others from our centers of tenderness is essential to intimate human communication. Erich Fromm has pointed out that while people are afraid of not being loved, the deeper and often more unconscious fear is the fear of loving. Maslow and Mittelman have defined love as "lowering one's defenses and becoming vulnerable to hurt."[6] But when people have been given messages while growing up that loving is too risky, then it is hard for them to feel that their lives will find fulfillment in developing loving relationships. The gospel certainly challenges mistaken beliefs about loving. The corrective truth can be found in the pattern of caring reflected in the gift of God's love in Jesus Christ and in the triumph of divine love over humankind's rejection of the Savior.

A story which translates into familial terms this theme of agape love as being central to the meaning of human experience depicts a little girl sitting on her mother's lap one day. She was looking up into her mother's face and said, "Mommy, you have a beautiful face, sparkling eyes, and lovely hair. But why are your hands and your arms so ugly?" The mother replied, "When you were just an infant, I left you sleeping alone in your crib one evening, the first time that I had ever left you alone in the house. I went down the street to visit a neighbor for a few minutes. While I was gone, our house caught on fire. When I realized that it was our house that was burning, I raced up the street. I dashed in through the flames and grabbed you up out of your crib. I held you close to me and tried to protect you from the flames with my hands and my arms. As we ran to safety, my hands and arms got badly burned.

That's why they are so ugly." With tears in her eyes, the little girl looked into her mother's face again and said, "Mommy, you have a beautiful face, sparkling eyes, and lovely hair. But your hands and your arms are the most beautiful of all."

Authentic love is beautiful. In spite of hurt and rejection love rises again. Loving and being loved is of the essence of one's true self and of fulfilling the unique image of God in oneself.

Family Dynamics as Religious Drama

The family is an interacting unit where theological meanings and religious values are played out generally without any conscious designation of either religious terminology or theological constructs. While affirming psychological and sociological perspectives on the family, I believe it can also be helpful to understand the family system as implicitly living out its own unique, profound religious drama.

Family therapy is basically an intervention into a religious drama being enacted in the home. Family therapists, who for a long time have been aware that they were dealing with value, meaning, and belief systems, have nevertheless not conceptualized family dynamics as a *religious* drama. While Nathan Ackerman in the early years of family therapy conceptualized the identified patient as the family "scapegoat," and people have noted the religious roots and meaning of that term, there has been very little research done to demonstrate that family therapy is also working with a covert theological system of profound religious themes and myths central to the life, growth, and homeostasis of the family.

Let us take a glimpse at some theological perspectives on the family's dynamics. First of all, let us look at the theme of atonement being acted out in family dynamics, especially in the role of the identified patient or scapegoat. The scapegoat is the one held responsible for the family problem. By being the family's burden bearer and the focus for conflict, the scapegoat seeks to secure atonement for the family by being its sacrificial lamb. Some family therapists speak to the scapegoated family member in a paradoxical way, saying, "You have been making a noble sacrifice on behalf of your family, protecting your parents from focusing on their marital and/or personal problems by deflecting attention to your problems. You are to be commended for such unselfishness and devoted sacrifice to other persons in your family."

The other members of the family may initially have difficulty with the therapist's re-labeling of the bad seed's role as being that of a noble sacrificer, and the individual will often disclaim that role. Underlying this concept of atonement seems to be the people's need for someone to be the burden bearer relieving the rest of the family of their guilt, conflict, and even sin. By crucifying a member of the family, individuals or marital dyads do not have to take responsibility for their own problems, since the focus can now be on the identified patient.

Such atonement in the family is a way of coping with idolatrous authority. If a child has very judgmental, critical, repressive parents, then he or she may opt for self-crucifixion through a variety of means, including psychological defenses distorting the natural and spontaneous self. Thus one sacrifices key elements in one's own personality for the sake of the family's ongoing life. Such defensive strategies are usually viewed through psychological perspectives, but they can also readily be understood through a theological perspective. It is well to note that most families would not conceptualize their dynamics in religious terms and may even consider themselves to be agnostic or atheistic, but that does not deny the reality of the theological dynamics which may be operative in the family. It is the implicit theological dynamics of the family that are relevant rather than the external, explicit religion articulated by members of the family.

A second issue in the religious drama of the family is the location of the family's household gods—its idols of power. Is someone in the family actually functioning as god or is that person only perceived by others as having divine power? It is true that parents do not necessarily arrogate divine power, but in their disciplining and attempting to organize and control the family, children may perceive them to be functioning as gods. In sculpturing a family, it can be interesting to ask where persons place God in the room. Where do they experience ultimate authority and power in the family? Does that ultimate authority affirm and bestow freedom to be to other members of the family, or does that authority constrict, control, and oppress others? It is also possible that an authority outside the nuclear family, such as a grandparent, may really be the family's locus of power.

The following theological perspectives on the Smith family may help to illustrate this idolatrous power in a home where children struggle with an authority of law versus the desire for an authority of grace.

In the Smith family, Mr. Smith is the central power figure, the dominant influence over his wife and their two teenage sons. Mr. Smith is a banker and a substantial member of First Church, serving on its board of trustees. He is forty-two years of age and has been successful in the financial world. His wife is thirty-eight and has focused her attention on the home and child-rearing. She defers to her husband and does not venture forth emotionally into the outside world. The two sons are Teddy, age sixteen and named after his father, and Bruce, who is age thirteen. Teddy is the identified patient because he has been rebellious and acting out, especially through dating a girl whom he got pregnant. Teddy and his father kept that a secret. The father handled that situation in his typical fashion, by not becoming emotionally or personally involved. He decided that the girl was of an inferior socioeconomic status compared to his son and paid one thousand dollars for the girl to have an abortion and for the relationship to terminate. Teddy wanted to marry the girl and take responsibility for the baby, and he was very resentful toward his father for using money to solve the situation.

Bruce was the so-called perfect son who had had only one escapade about five years ago, when he engaged in some vandalism at his school. On that occasion, however, the father was able to hide the information from the public by quickly paying for the damage. Bruce came to realize that he needed the acceptance of his parents, and therefore he decided to give up his search for independence and to conform to their expectations. Teddy had been worried about his brother Bruce because he felt that his brother gave up his freedom to be himself in order to preserve his place in the family. Teddy felt some sadness for his brother, as he felt that Bruce has lost real zest for living. The precipitating incident which initiated family counseling was that Teddy had run away for a few days and had just returned home. Teddy worried that, through hiring a family therapist, his father was once again using money to force a quick solution that would leave intact the family's power dynamics.

The other significant person in the life of this family had been a woman named Annie, who had been a kind of governess for the children for many years until she died five years ago. She had been a warm and affirming person with the boys, and they had related to her as a very positive surrogate parent. In fact, Annie's death appeared to be the precipitating event for Bruce's delinquency and Teddy's rebellion. Annie had a way of being open with the boys' discipline problems, dealing with the brothers effectively and justly and buffering their father's harsh and judgmental attitude. With her death, however, there was no longer an advocate in the family for the boys and thus the affirmation for their individuality was absent.

From one theological perspective, Teddy was functioning in terms of the Protestant principle of justification by grace. He was protesting and attacking the family ethos of living under the law and the pharisaical expectation that family acceptance was merited by appropriately fulfilling its laws and arbitrary rules. His acting out was a cry for acceptance of the person he was. Naturally, the family saw Teddy as the evil or destructive one rather than as a kind of Pauline figure who was struggling against the law and for the good news of acceptance. In this regard Annie had been a Christ-figure—she integrated love with firmness. The boys experienced Annie as one who cared for them, who affirmed them, and who would be with them in the midst of their struggles. When she died it was as if the good world ended for the boys. Vulnerability to a "bad god" and the lack of advocacy of a Christ-figure during childhood often make it difficult for adults to have much sense of Christ as Savior, Messiah, and Rescuer. It also leaves children with a distorted definition of self that makes it extremely difficult for them to identify themselves as the beloved child of the Divine Parent.

A third way of looking at the religious drama of the family is to investigate the secular scriptures by which the family lives. One can understand a lot about the implicit religion of a family through an examination of the rules, laws, injunctions, and directives that permeate the family, particularly those governing child-rearing practices. We have previously noted how such secular scriptures as "Do not feel," "Do not feel anger," and "Do not feel sadness" operate as though they came down from the holy mountain, and it would be an unpardonable sin to violate such a law.

Secular scriptures carrying such divine imperatives often play havoc with the self-esteem of children in the family. The impact of the idea that "children should be seen and not heard," which at times is communicated even more intensely as "Do not be," is devastating to children living under that destructive law. Such harmful values and beliefs can be readily understood as false religious teachings even though individuals in that family do not articulate them as specifically religious. However, in some instances parents bring in the power of the church and the threat of a wrathful God to reinforce these controlling and repressive secular scriptures.

My contention is that we need to help people to uncover and see the self-defeating nature of the oppressive beliefs and values by which they are living in their families. In religious terminology, people need to confess, own, and repent of the secular scriptures by which they are living and which they accept as the gospel truth. Before persons are able to move beyond those lies which they have baptized as truths, they may need help in viewing the guiding principles of the family as lies and distortions.

It is also interesting to note how an appreciation of family dynamics as an implicit religious drama may be helpful in working with a conservative, closed, religious family system. These can be difficult to enter unless a counselor has some appreciation for the dynamic meaning of the rigid religious conceptualizations of the family. For example, in many closed family systems justified by religious injunctions, there is little or no tolerance for autonomy for the growing children. Conformity to the family and the church value system is powerfully imprinted on the children, and children pay a high emotional price if they seek to move towards some freedom of their own personhood.

The pastoral counselor can find creative fulfillment in utilizing theology as a vantage point to understand themes and to intervene therapeutically in the implicit religious dramas played out in marital and family systems.

The Operational Theology of the "Common Cold"— Depression

One evening, while working with another pastoral psychotherapist in a group therapy setting, I listened to a woman who was depressed depict the shattering of her hopes by picturing them as being smashed on the floor and splintering into millions of pieces. To my amazement, my co-therapist said to her: "Good, just let them lie there on the floor. It can be a good thing to have your false hopes smashed. If you don't pick them up and try to put them together again the same old way, you may be free to seek and define an authentic and unbreakable hope." It took me a while to understand that this interpretation was a creative intervention in the woman's life. My colleague had seen correctly that the woman's earthly hopes had been operating as her means of salvation. It was as if the co-therapist's vision had been of smashing the idol of the golden calf so that this woman might be open to the true hope in the living God. The Danish theologian Søren Kierkegaard's insight is relevant here: "Earthly hope must be killed; only then can one be saved by true hope."[1]

Hope is central to vital life. Hope that survives the vicissitudes of life is dynamically linked to the Eternal. While it is a normal part of human development to attach our hopes to significant persons and to such created things as health, money, status, security, sexuality, and maturity, Christian theology has long taught that the only basis for enduring and authentic hope is in relationship to God who is the creator, life-giver, savior, and redeemer. Such hope may be grounded in optimism and trust deriving from a loving and constructively affirming early childhood environment. If we are to transcend despair, those penultimate hopes must be transformed. Christian theology has taught that when ultimate hope is attached to a created thing and not to the Creator, this is an idolatry leaving one open to disillusionment and despair. Paul says, "For in this hope we were saved. Now hope that is seen is not hope. For who hopes for what he sees. But if we hope for what we do not see, we wait for it with patience" (Rom. 8:24-25 RSV). A contemporary statement of this view of hope comes from James L. Muyskens:

> Like faith, hope is the attitude of the adventurer and discoverer, not the technician. Like faith, hope affirms a way out in spite of obstacles. Christian hope, like faith, is the freedom to decipher the signs of the Resurrection under the apparently contradictory evidence of death.[2]

Idolatry underlies much of the depression seen by pastoral counselors, particularly in those clients with neurotic problems. Here, I am conceiving of depression as "unhope" based on faulty perceptions of ultimate reality and one's own identity, and on an implicit belief system holding that crucifixion has overcome resurrection, that death has overcome life, that evil has overcome good, that the demonic has overcome God. People become vulnerable to depression and despair when their hopes have been placed on false absolutes and when their own abilities and resources to save and atone for themselves are breaking down and are not producing the desired results. Erroneous belief systems, distorted world views, and idolatrous misperceptions of reality are key concepts in understanding, preventing, and treating depression.

The typical neurotic pattern for depression is built around a false image of ultimate authority which has failed to validate, mirror, affirm, and confirm a person's unique worth. Therefore, there is a basic anxiety and insecurity about one's place in the world, and one makes neurotic adaptations and accommodations to try to placate or manipulate the "bad god" into granting the gift of caring, stroking, and approving of the individual. That approach of trying to turn a "bad god" into the good God by the manipulation of one's selfhood is always doomed to failure. The Christian affirmation is that, ontologically, each person is already grounded in love, acceptance, and grace. Therefore, hope is already present, because one belongs to that new creation given by God in Christ which affirms that, in spite of all of the crucifixions, dark days, and Golgothas, the only true, ultimate reality is that of Resurrection, renewal, and the victory of life and love.

"Depression has been called the world's number one health problem. In fact, depression is so widespread it is considered the common cold of psychiatric disturbances."[3] Much research is now being done on the etiology and treatment of depression in an effort to combat this epidemic. Acknowledgment is granted for possible genetic causes, biochemical linkages, sociogenic theories, et cetera. Scientists are using increasingly sophisticated research tools to explore the possibility that imbalances in brain chemistry cause depression. Anti-depressant drugs administered and monitored by competent medical supervisors may be very helpful to selected depressed persons. However, it is imperative to remember that there are many unanswered questions about the causation and treatment of various types of depression. My theory is that a theological listening perspective and treatment philosophy regarding depression may be another significant way to minister to our age of depression.

Cognitive therapists such as Aaron T. Beck and David D. Burns, in considering depression a disturbance in one's world view and thinking, point the way toward clinical theology. These therapists suggest that negative thoughts, usually based on gross distortions of reality, form the basis for most depression. People *feel* depressed because of their pervasive negative *thinking*. These researchers on depression are coming to the conclusion of the wisdom of the ages: "For as he thinketh in his heart, so is he" (Prov. 23:7 KJV). According to these cognitive therapists, a depressed person has a negative conceptual triad: (1) a negative evaluation of self, with overwhelming self-blame, (2) a negative evaluation and expectation of the environment, making the person helpless, and (3) a negative assessment of the future, leading to hopelessness. We can recast this negative conceptual triad into a theological form that, while not exhaustive, is illustrative.

1. *Negative Self-Image.* A person who is depressed may not experience his or her identity as a beloved child of God. Depressed persons may not affirm their worth as having been created in the image of God. That person may not profoundly experience God's forgiveness and acceptance. One may believe in the bad news *about* oneself and may not trust in the good news *for* oneself. The depressed individual may not have internalized that, while one is unlovable, one is still loved and that, while one is unacceptable, one is still accepted. He or she may not have grasped the truth that at the core of reality there is a dynamic, caring Heart which takes the initiative to love, affirm, forgive, and sustain. A person with depression may not believe that "we love because he first loved us" (I John 4:19 RSV). A person who is depressed may not internalize the reality that in this world of tribulation, sin, and struggle it is not necessary to make atonement

by depression and self-blame. Such an individual may not be aware that the Center of the Universe is not interested in condemnation but rather is actively involved in redemption. Thus, if one has taken one's definition of identity and self from a false god, then one is extremely vulnerable to depression. Here again we can understand how a case of mistaken identity leads to despair.

2. *Negative Evaluation of the Environment.* People struggling with depression may not have deeply experienced a dynamically supportive community of faith, a sustaining fellowship of caring persons to provide the emotional and spiritual supplies to empower him or her for abundant living. They may have no sense of the possibilities of being energized by the presence of the Holy Spirit. People who are so low that they are looking up at the bottom may have no sensitivity to the whole creation as the gift of a beneficent Creator seeking to provide the necessary resources to nurture and sustain life. There may be no sense of a covenant community working together to effectively promote social justice and liberation from depression. There may be a lack of affirmation in the heart of the truth, "in the world, you shall have tribulation; but be of good cheer, I have overcome the world" (John 16:33 RSV).

3. *Negative Assessment of the Future.* Depressed people's eschatological outlook may be that evil reigns supreme and always will, that the devil is victorious over God, that hostility and indifference are more powerful than love, that crucifixion is

the last word and resurrection is impossible, that history stops on Calvary with gloom and doom, and there is no Easter Sunday bringing new life. Despairing people may live entombed in an encapsulated world. They may not experience the hope, promise, and joy of either Eternal Love or eternal life.

Burns has an interesting analogy for the pastoral counselor interested in transforming people's depression into hope.

> Depression is always the result of mental 'static' distortions. Your blue moods can be compared to the scratchy music coming from a radio that is not properly tuned to the station. The problem is not that the tubes or transistors are blown out or defective, or that the signal from the radio station is distorted as a result of bad weather. You just simply have to adjust the dials. When you learn to bring about this mental tuning, the music will come through clearly again and your depression will lift.[4]

Pastoral counselors can easily agree with this kind of thinking, pointing to the theological importance of being centered, aligned with one's deepest self, and tuned in to transcendent realities. It is important, however, not to fall into the temptation to oversimplify the causes and treatment of depression with naive religious cliches and inspirational religious prescriptions. The "stinking thinking" of the depressed and their idolatrous world views are not cured by the inspirational religious message taped for telephone callers looking for a band-aid treatment for their depression.

A theological listening perspective encourages the pastoral counselor to help clients examine their twin idolatry, with its negative view of God, of self, and of the world which so constricts and depresses their lives. Some suggestions for a therapeutic approach are as follows:

1. Help the depressed to review the secular scriptures and secular prayers connected with their depression. With appropriate timing, bring the creative teachings of the Christian faith to bear in relevant ways upon their erroneous views of reality. Verbally and nonverbally, bring the story of the good news to address their world governed by bad news.

2. Think of depression not as something that goes on solely in the head of a single individual. Be aware that a person can be in a depressed role in a family or an organization because others have hidden emotional investments in that person carrying the group's depressive burden. Keep working with a systems orientation with persons who are depressed, helping to mobilize the caring network of persons around him or her. If there is no natural support network then help form a group around an isolated person who is suffering from depression.

3. Seek to understand and affirm how difficult it is for many people to move out from underneath the dark clouds of depression. For

decades they may have been accustomed to finding their place in a world of gloom and doom. It is often frightening for them to give up their familiar attachments to idols, negative world views, and customary ways of thinking, feeling, and doing. Some people find it risky to move out of their depressed world into a new creation, to transcend the bad news with the good news, or to grow from a negative identification of self to acceptance of one's significant worth by the Ultimate Guarantor of human worth.

4. In intervening in depression from a theological perspective, do not induce guilt feelings by communicating critically, "If you would only straighten out your thinking and your lousy world view, then you'd get over being depressed." The pastoral counselor needs to be careful not to function with a critical superego during confrontations.

5. Help people to find or rediscover a why, a meaning, a goal, a dream for living. Victor Frankl and others have pointed out the central importance of having meaning and purpose in life so that people do not withdraw from living and become depressed. Howard Thurman said it well: "As long as a man has a dream in his heart, he cannot lose the significance of living."[5] In this regard, the pastoral psychotherapist may need to occasionally reaffirm for himself or herself those beliefs which proclaim

hope in the midst of adversity. For me, two passages of scripture have been particularly helpful: "And if Christ be not risen . . . your faith is also vain" (I Cor. 15:14 KJV) and

> I have become absolutely convinced that neither death nor life, neither messenger of Heaven nor monarch of earth, neither what happens today nor what may happen tomorrow, neither a power from on high nor a power from below, nor anything else in God's whole world has any power to separate us from the love of God in Christ Jesus, our Lord (Rom. 8:38-39 JPB).

While pastoral counselors may focus theologically mainly on intrapsychic and interpersonal issues in dealing with depression, it is also important for us to keep alive the struggle for social justice, since all kinds of institutional oppression (racism, sexism, ageism, classism) naturally place people in situations in which they are more vulnerable to depression. To labor solely to change people's intrapsychic world views, helping them adapt to an unjust society, would be a cop-out on our responsibilities to transform society as well as individuals. Oppression is intimately connected with depression. Pastoral counselors and the church must work to change both the outer as well as inner social structures in the process of ministering to depressed persons.

The Fear of Hoping

While religious counselors usually think of hope in a positive context, our clinical experiences confirm that some people look at hope negatively. Many people's hopes have been so disappointed and hurt, particularly in intimate relationships, that they now are afraid to hope. Failure of hope may cause some to echo Nietzsche's sentiment, "Hope is the worst of evils, for it prolongs the torment of man."[6] The fear of hoping often has its roots in this failure of objects of hope to fulfill promises. Frequently, significant others in whom one has invested certain hopes and to whom one is vulnerable have proven to be untrustworthy. The hurt and rejection received at their hands may be translated into a fear of trusting and hoping in other persons and even in God. To hope again is to be vulnerable to further disappointment and to despair; thus some people decide that it is best not to hope, in order to protect themselves from further hurt and grief. This idea is conveyed in a contemporary bumper sticker: "Since I gave up hope, I feel much better."

Hope in No Hope

Ironically, some people may feel that their hope is in having no hope. Usually these persons have been let down in various ways, and they believe that it is better to live with no hope than to reach out for the possibility of a dependable, good relationship, only to be disappointed and hurt even worse than before. This hope in no hope is clearly demonstrated in the following dream of a young adult woman who had been severely hurt emotionally in her relationships in her family of origin and again in her failing marriage. In this dream, which was presented in a group and dealt with mainly by my co-therapist, the woman placed herself in a glass room like a shower, with the handle to the room's only door on the outside. There was a crack in the glass of one of the room's corners, and through this crack came some spiders. She was lying on the floor and the spiders began to crawl over her. Though she screamed for help, no one would come to open the door.

As one approach (among many) to the interpretation of this dream my colleague utilized the manipulation of the dream symbols to ask her to imagine that the spiders had changed into kittens. She resisted this suggestion intensely, saying that she could not allow such an imaginary change. Besides, the spiders weren't too bad to endure, for if she changed the spiders into kittens and the kittens turned out to be evil, then she would be at her rope's end. She preferred to live with her perspective that the world is hostile rather than risk the possibility of another hope being shattered.

Pastoral counselors may also find this fear of hoping a key dynamic in certain marital conflicts. An unhappy spouse may have given up working for any reconciliation in the marital relationship because he or she has reached the end of the tether in hoping for change in the mate and the relationship. To hope again in the marriage would be to become vulnerable to another deep disappointment. The wife of a salesman in a marriage full of disharmony began to revitalize her hopes during a week when her husband was away on business. Her hopes were quickly shattered when he returned home in a rage, his temper erupting in all directions. After this experience, she anguished: "It's really better not to hope at all. I only feel worse after my hopes have been built up and they are shattered. I am worse off than when I started." Thus again and again in various counseling situations pastoral counselors may hear Shelley's theme: "Worse than despair, worse than the bitterness of death, is hope."[7]

Hope in Non-Being

While some people seek to protect themselves from the risk of further disappointed hopes by having none, others handle their fear of hoping by centering their expectations on those things we would usually consider the antithesis of hope. That is, their hope is really attached to aspects of non-being. The world has become so overwhelming to some that they feel their only possible deliverance from such an earthly hell is to cut themselves off from the realities of painful human life by annihilating their being. Going crazy or seeking death may become two objects of hope for those who feel they can bear no more.

A hardworking laywoman tells a story of having been so overwhelmed by family responsibilities, sickness, and church conflicts that she lost all hope. In her despair she contemplated how she could get out from under all of the burdens. A dream turned the tide for her. In the dream her suitcases were packed and she was just getting ready to leave for a mental hospital. Her husband was with her. His attitude was one of feeling sorry for her but accepting the fact that she must go to the hospital. Certain things in her life that meant a great deal to her, such as her work, caring for her children, and being a companion to her husband then passed in review. The dream helped her to realize that her hope of mental illness as a way out of her predicament would yield more negative consequences than constructive results. Thus she was able to give up her hope of mental illness as the solution to her situation.

In a similar vein, pastoral counselors encounter people who view suicide as the only avenue of deliverance from certain pains of human life. Since ultimate reality seems so negative and there are no resources in or around oneself to cope with the sufferings, struggles, and problems of life, one's hope may be fastened on death as the only way out. It may also seem the only way to destroy the "bad god" and the "bad me"—as the only way to conquer the twin idolatry.

This resembles the "sickness unto death" of which Kierkegaard wrote so penetratingly. It is the "attempt to maintain oneself by sinking still deeper."[8] It is a closing of the door to "everything which is of the nature of repentance and everything which is of the nature of grace."[9] This despair is experienced in an idolatrous context where the ultimate authority is hostile toward the person and there is no superior or divine power strong enough, capable enough, or caring enough to protect or rescue the person, so that she or he enters into despair. This despair is not oriented toward a nothingness. The despair is over feeling the superiority of the power of the idol, which symbolically represents the power of the demonic over the power of God. Paul Pruyser offers substantial support for this point of view:

> I do not think that Luther had an "unimaginable horror" over nothingness, nor that he threw his inkwell at non-being. His 'void of nothingness,' like the 'dark night of the soul' of many mystics, was filled with visions of psychically real, almost substantial, actually threatening beings such as the devil and his cohorts. The existential choice situation for Kierkegaard was not between something or nothing, but between God and the devil, God and flesh, good and evil portrayed, between becoming one type of person or another type of person. If there is a passionate experience of passion there is always an object of passion, not that one is always conscious of this object. We must maintain, however, the hypothesis that an object is there, somewhere in one's memory. Contrary to Kierkegaard's verbal formulations, dread is not produced by nothing. It is produced by a threatening substance or the image thereof.[10]

Unhope

The fear of hoping and the desire for annihilation of one's being is often connected to a subtle process of elevating the hostile and the demonic to the throne of the absolute. Persons who have experienced a shattering of penultimate hopes may conclude that evil and negativity reign supreme, and that there is no Ultimate Good in whom to place their hopes. The breakdown of hopes in human relationships may lead to the generalization that the perceived Heart of Reality is not affirming, trustworthy, loving, or hopeful. The pastoral counselor needs to be aware that the despairing person may view the core of the universe as being against him or herself. One may have projected onto the Ultimate some image growing out of hurtful human relationships and experiences, so that a false god of vast negative powers is imagined to be supreme. In theological language, the powers that fill life with crucifixions are experienced as real and ultimate, and the power that can salvage, rescue, heal, and resurrect is experienced as false and illusory.

Apparently meaningless pain which continues for an extended time tends to raise doubts that there is a loving advocate and savior who can rescue people from the despairing hell. Helmut Thielicke addresses the power of the internal tempter who utilizes the factors of pain and time to convince people that God is not really a good, loving, powerful, and rescuing advocate.

> And so the tempter, when he proposes to attack in earnest, allows the suffering to exceed the limits of what a person can regard as reasonable. The moment at which one thinks it must stop because one has learned enough is precisely the moment at which it does not cease; it goes on senselessly. Time is the most uncanny minister of this prince of darkness. Time saps our resistance, not because it goes on so long but because it is so meaningless.[11]

Despair is related to the breakdown of one's own defensive strategy of salvation, which has not been effective in providing the fulfillment in life that the person has desired. When the idolatrous patterns are ineffective, then one is vulnerable to despair and unhope. Thomas Merton, in a contemplative vein, writes of this experience:

> Despair is the absolute extreme of self-love. It is reached when a man deliberately turns his back on all help from anyone else in order to taste the rotten luxury of knowing himself to be lost. In every man there is hidden some root of despair because in every man there is pride that vegetates and springs weeds and rank flowers of self-pity as soon as our own resources fail us. But because our own resources inevitably fail us, we are all more or less subject to discouragement and to despair. Despair is the ultimate development of a pride so great and so stiff-necked that it selects the absolute misery of damnation rather than accept happiness from the hands of God and thereby acknowledge that He is above us and that we are not capable of fulfilling our destiny by ourselves. But a man who is truly humble cannot despair because in the humble man there is no longer any such thing as self-pity.[12]

Many clinicians would agree that depression is full of defiance and highly narcissistic. Some would speak more theologically of how despair involves an unwillingness to be open to receiving grace. Daim writes:

> Despair as an outgrowth of radical and total doubt implies first of all an element of "losing patience."

Despair is thus always also "impatience," that is, the "inability to wait," when the psyche finds itself face to face with a power which can but must not heed the call for help. Despair implies secondly pride and arrogance deriving from an indignant revolt against the actually demanded dependency on grace. This, as a matter of fact, amounts to a revolt against salvation as such and is thus a rebellion against that which might aid in leading from discord and doubt to harmony and trusting acceptance. We can see then clearly that despair always includes the elements of impatience and revolt, as well as the lack of faith, hope and love. Despair in short is essentially an unwillingness to believe in saving grace.[13]

The Transformation of Unhope

Thielicke suggests, "The real therapy appears when one begins to realize that this world is loved by an everlasting Heart and that therefore we are summoned to say 'yes' to life."[14] The pastoral counselor is to mediate this love of the Eternal Heart through providing an affirming, holding environment in the therapeutic relationship with the client or client system. The pastoral counselor needs to have integrated this good news so that it is mediated implicitly in client interactions. The pastoral psychotherapist can only try to share this gift of grace with clients. He or she cannot knock the defensive doors down.

A simple story (reportedly from one of Charles Spurgeon's sermons) illustrates how many people expect the negative to be awaiting them at every turn. An old woman was so poor that she often lay in bed for a large part of the day in order to keep warm. One day her minister called with a gift of money for her. He knocked several times at the door but received no answer. A couple of days later he met her in the street and told her of his visit. "Ah," she said, "I was in bed. The door was locked. You see, I had no money and I thought it was the landlord come to collect the rent." People who have been hurt deeply at the core of their lives may not expect or hope for a God of grace to be knocking at the door of their hearts. They may have made an idol of the negativity which they experienced. They may have sought to make themselves their own savior in the vicissitudes of life, without coming to grips with the fact that our own human resources inevitably fail us.

Therapeutic work with such depressed persons may be long and hard. But the despairing or unhoping ones are not to be blamed or condemned; rather, they are to be understood as suffering from idolatry and the failure of their strategies for saving themselves. Thus having no hope or placing one's hope in self-annihilation may be seen as an expression of an erroneous belief in a false, negative absolute or in dependency on unhoping as the only way of deliverance from life's burdens. The pastoral counseling of despairing individuals may be a long and complex process in which the therapist and a fellowship of caring persons mediate the good news that while there *is* tribulation in this world, we do not need to lose heart or hope, for the powers of the world have been overcome in Christ and the victory is revealed in the Crucifixion-Resurrection event.

Amidst the intricacies of working with people suffering from depression, the pastoral counselor will also need to keep in mind the perspective of the twin idolatry of the false absolute that dominates people's world views and the failure of the strategy of self-deliverance through various atonements, leading to depression. It is to be hoped that over a period of time the counselee will gain a new perception of ultimate reality and develop a genuine hope in the victorious God in Christ. As Thielicke expressed this truth:

> When a person sees the fact of Jesus Christ and it dawns on one that the universe is fatherly and that one is loved, one loses one's fear, not that all the oppressing and depressing powers are banished from one's life . . . but that they no longer have any power over one.[15]

Truly, operational Christian theology offers much hope for the healing of depression, the common cold of emotional problems.

Self-justification Versus Justification by Faith Through Grace

"*And please protect me from the appearance of wrongdoing.*"

Drawing by Lorenz; © 1982 The New Yorker Magazine, Inc.

The above cartoon depicts one dimension of the human striving for self-justification. We often seek to promote a favorable review of ourselves to others and to our own internal critic by employing various strategies of self-justification to maximize our self-image. We often need to protect ourselves from feelings of vulnerability and inadequacy, and to preserve our good appearance by pretense, masks, and excuses.

The Longing to be Made Right

Le Roy Aden writes: "People have an intense longing to be made right. They may want to get right with themselves, others, and/or with God, but in any case they feel, however vaguely, that there is something wrong with them and they desire, however fervently, to become acceptable."[1] These attempts to be the source of one's own righteousness can appear on the surface to go in two opposite directions. Some people try to be made right through their own efforts at good and noble works, so that their praiseworthy performance will bring them the validation they seek. On the other hand, others turn against themselves in negative and self-destructive ways as though self-negation and the crucifixion of their own personalities would be an acceptable atonement to get them into the relationships that they seek.

This longing to be made right has three major facets:

> Like any theater, there are three basic components to the self-image—the actor (in this case, oneself), the performance (how one behaved in a particular situational setting), and the audience (a combination of others and oneself). The self-image is thus defined as an actor's mental picture of his or her performance in a particular situation before an audience.[2]

Self-justification involves the actor in life playing to audiences without (others and/or God) and within so that through one's performance one may experience self-acceptance. It is imperative to remember that underneath prideful good works, self-destructive behaviors, and egoistic attempts to be superhumanly good, there is a fundamental longing to be made right with the ultimate source of life.

Defensive Strategies of Self-justification

Self-atoning strategies of life reflect the second phase of the double idolatry in which one seeks to maneuver or manipulate, however unconsciously, the negative ultimate authority into granting one some measure of approval, acceptance, and forgiveness. The nature and character of the idol itself plays a significant part in determining the atonement strategy and self-justifying behaviors used to placate or please the idol.

The Reverend Jack Sims struggled almost weekly with his schedule, especially in terms of time for sermon preparation. There was always so much to do in his parish that on many Saturday evenings and a few early Sunday mornings he found himself desperately trying to pull together his thoughts for the sermon. "What's wrong with me?" he fumed. "I've got to get my act together. I've failed myself, the congregation, and God by not getting this sermon done again. I've got to do better next week." However, Jack's good intentions did not seem to alter his behavior much from week to week. He still wrestled with guilt over his inability to finish his sermon without a last-minute deadline hanging over his head. For years he was stuck in this torturous pattern.

Through a crisis experience that pushed Jack into therapy, he discovered that his difficulty with sermon preparation was only symptomatic of a far more pervasive spiritual and emotional problem. Jack found that he was caught between two parts of himself (called subpersonalities or subselves) in regard to sermon preparation. Jack experienced the pressure of writing his sermon as a demand that came out of his internalized "Taskmaster" subpersonality, which gave him the injunction, "You must, you ought to, and you should write your sermon early in the week." However, there was a polar opposite subpersonality called "the Procrastinator" which resisted all shoulds and demands. The Procrastinator responded passively but powerfully with, "Hell, no. You're not ordering me around." Sermon preparation was like a badminton shuttlecock being hit back and forth between the two courts of the Taskmaster and the Procrastinator. Every demand to write was met with resistance to it. Only the "demon of the deadline" enabled him to complete his preparation.

In therapy, Jack discovered something underneath these two subpersonalities. As a child growing up, Jack learned that he was given attention and approval for achievements and for helpfulness and thoughtfulness toward others. He found himself valued when he met the needs and expectations of others. He did not experience, however, that acceptance and love were available to him for just being himself. Jack Sims felt that good deeds, thoughtful acts, or successful achievements earned him approval. Before the age of five, Jack had learned the lesson that he was justified as a human being by negating his own needs and feelings and by being the "nice guy" who took care of others at the expense of his authentic self. Jack had developed a "neurotic pastoral identity" as a little boy; he learned that he was of worth only if he was ministering to others and discounting himself. That pattern persisted into adulthood.

Jack did not experience grace being mediated to him by the significant others in his childhood world. Even as a young child he perceived authority as undependable and felt that he could only depend upon himself and his own resources and achievements. His unconscious strategy to secure self-esteem was to try to gain the approval of those around him, whom he did not really trust, by doing for them in pleasing ways. Deep inside, however, Jack felt resentment at not being accepted for himself, and it manifested itself in various covert, passive ways. It naturally followed that he projected onto God the unreliable authority images of his childhood, and he tried to manipulate the "unloving and unaccepting god" by being a good and hard-working minister as he had been a good and self-sacrificing child.

Jack was caught in two idolatries. First, he had misperceived the nature of God in his own life and substituted the undependable, ungraceful parental images as ultimate authority. Then to placate that authority and to gain approval from that god, Jack moved to the second idolatry of crucifying his own God-given nature as a way of seeking atonement. The repression of central elements in his own personality was an unconscious messianic act designed to save himself from alienation from the love that he needed. But ironically, in becoming his own "christ," he was alienated from the real Christ who had already made the supreme sacrifice of love on Jack's behalf, so that he could truly know atonement.

Jack needed to confess both idolatries. He had to struggle to believe in that Divine Love, so different from the conditional love that he had known in growing up. He had to give up attempting to control that false god by seeking to earn approval. He had to learn something of the radical love of God which initiated caring for Jack. He had to learn that he could trust in God's graceful love and that justification is a gift, not a demand for performance. The theology of justification by faith through grace had to change from being solely an intellectual concept, something true for his parishioners but not for him, to being an internalized experience of God's love initiating on Jack's behalf and seeking him out at any price to reunite him with his Creator. In time the Good News became his good news. Jack moved personally and professionally from a religion of good works and of seeking to fulfill the law to a profound experience of a trusting relationship with God in Christ.

The above illustration can be repeated in thousands of variations in the lives of clergy and laity hungering for love and grace but trapped in the psychic idolatry of self-defeating strategies to validate and justify themselves. Experiences in the childhood family with significant authority figures are often critical in determining whether people develop relationships of trust and grace or whether they become involved in psychological and spiritual patterns in which they do not feel affirmed, validated, or accepted unless they destructively manipulate their personalities.

Paul Tillich has particularly noted that accepting a person in the counseling relationship is a paradigm of the good news of God's acceptance of people even when they are unacceptable. Tillich suggested that the reclamation of the centrality of the doctrine of "justification by faith through grace" (the good news that one who feels unworthy of being accepted by God can be certain that one is accepted) has largely been due to the field of psychotherapy which has emphasized the importance of acceptance in the counseling relationship.

> The psychoanalytic pattern of a non-judging and non-directing acceptance of the mentally disturbed became the model for Christian counseling, and through counseling, for teaching, and through teaching, for theological inquiry. Present theology can say again that acceptance by God of one who is not able to accept oneself is the center of the Christian message and the theological foundation of preaching and pastoral counseling. . . . One can say that in spite of

Freud's own anti-religious assertions, the transformation of the intellectual climate by him was the greatest
intellectual support for a rediscovery of the central
Christian message, the good news of acceptance.[3]

Pastoral counselors need to appreciate the extent
to which people caught in bondage to idolatrous
images of God are living out their lives in
accordance with false laws and seeking atonement
through justification by good works. These persons
are living by the secular scripture, "My yoke is
difficult and my burden is heavy." Counselors can
be extremely helpful in understanding counselees
who may be caught up in self-justification because
they have not been able to experience and receive
God's grace.

Oftentimes these people are responsible, hard-
working church members who take themselves and
their religious obligations very seriously. They tend
to operate mainly out of the Parent and Adult ego
states, and they find the spontaneity and fun-loving
dimensions of the Child ego state foreign to their
experience. They often function rationally, logically,
and intellectually, with little contact with the intuitive
and emotional parts of their personality. They have
not been able to integrate the metaphorical and
symbolic thinking of the right brain with the
cognitive approach of the left brain. These people are
subject to the emotional and physical problems of
those who experience ultimate reality as so demanding that they have to work out their own acceptance
by justifying themselves with superhuman efforts.

Pastoral counselors are on the forefront of understanding the universal, profound human need for validation that is neither earned nor merited. Self-justification sought through various achievements proves to be a hollow success because one does not experience that the true self is loved and accepted for itself. A prayer expressing the need for divine love which affirms and accepts people's uniqueness begins with the phrase, "O Thou who lovest each one of us as though each of us was Thine only child." Each human heart yearns for that Divine Guarantor who affirms the specialness, the uniqueness of the individual.

People often have a difficult time trusting that there can be unearned acceptance when in their most significant relationships they have had to try to *win* approval and acceptance through achievement and other adaptive behaviors. This can lead to pride, which says, "I'd rather do it myself," resulting in a barrier to receiving grace. When people lack sound experiences of trust and grace, it is usually difficult for them to receive the gospel of grace deeply into their hearts. Often, it is only when people experience grace being mediated through other persons that they can be open to the possibility of divine grace. Reuel Howe was fond of saying that it takes "person healing" to help overcome "person hurts."[4]

Pastoral counselors should not be quick to judge or confront in a condemnatory way when they discover in themselves or in counselees the dynamics of idolatry that cause reliance on self-justification rather than grace. People need an atmosphere of acceptance in order to explore, acknowledge, claim, and confess the subjective reasons why they may have needed to choose such a spiritually sabotaging pattern. The important thing is not to condemn oneself or another for what in many ways may have been a necessary adaptation to ensure survival in one's childhood family. Too often when people discover and confess an idolatrous pattern by which they are living, a critical part of themselves says, "I shouldn't be who I am. I am bad. I am a failure." Such condemnation may only lock them further into self-condemnation rather than opening the doors to forgiveness and reconciliation. Thus the pastoral counselor's understanding and acceptance of the discovery of self-justifying patterns may lead people beyond self-denunciation into the experience of grace.

Opening Doors to Grace

There are a variety of ways by which the pastoral counselor may help people move to acceptance of themselves as beloved persons. Let us look at a few illustrations involving pastoral counselors working in different ways to fulfill this task. The first way is by helping a counselee name the oppressive idol causing him or her to live out a self-justifying life. People may give the name of the true God to that idol image; the naming of the idol may help to lessen its power.

For example, an older gentleman in a local parish was made a deacon because of his religiosity and hard work for the church. What he disclosed to the pastoral counselor in private, however, was that he was tormented inside by feelings that he could never do enough to please God. He was always driven to do more and to do it better to gain God's approval for his life. The counselor was aware that this monstrous image of a demanding God who could never be pleased was radically different from the God revealed in Jesus Christ, so he questioned the deacon concerning his mental representation of God. Finally the man identified and labeled his God image as the "Demander." He realized that the Demander originated in his punitive and blaming father whom he could never please. Whereas he had formerly experienced his guilt as being unable to please this wrathful god, he now saw that his true guilt was that he had been invested in an idolatrous projection of his father's image onto the Godhead. With the help of the counselor, the deacon was gradually able to believe that the nature of God was full of grace instead of demanding wrath.

Naming of the idolatrous, self-justifying patterns utilized to appease the false ultimate authority may help to free one to be open to being justified, confirmed, and validated by love and grace. For example, an executive had been plagued by bouts of depression due to the exhaustion following intense, prolonged periods of hard work with little sleep. His self-diagnosis prior to therapy had always been depression and burnout. However, a more detailed investigation revealed a fear of going crazy or disintegrating as his beloved older brother had when the businessman was just an adolescent. Since he had often been compared to his brother prior to the brother's permanent institutionalization, he worried even more about losing his sanity.

To ward off the danger of going crazy, the executive had tried to function at superhuman levels of accomplishment. There was a neurotic bargain with a "bad god": "If I work to the point of exhaustion, then you will keep me from going crazy like my brother did." So the bouts of depression and burnout were like atonement offerings at the altar of the gods to keep craziness from being inflicted upon him. Better to be depressed and burned out than to be crazy. Naming his defensive strategy to protect himself from insanity enabled him to see the absurdity of his bargain and to become freer to choose to live in a grace-filled world.

Another point for therapeutic intervention in the lives of people struggling with self-justification can be the secular scriptures. The counselor can help identify lies functioning as divine truths and seriously limiting a person's life. One example comes from the life of a woman who had completed her homemaking tour of duty and had chosen to adventure into a new realm. She decided to enter seminary in order to prepare herself for ministry.

During the second semester of her theological education, she encountered a course and a male professor which clashed with her emotional chemistry. Clearly, the only rational and responsible decision to make in the situation was to drop that course. Everything within her, including her somatic reactions, indicated that she should withdraw from the course. However, a significant element of her childhood belief system stood as a towering barrier forbidding her to do so. Through conversations with her pastoral counselor she realized that as a child she had been taught the secular scripture, "Everything that comes to you in life is from the providential hand of God. Therefore you must always endure whatever comes, as that is the will of God for you. You will be a failure if you choose to say 'no' to any burden. You are not to ask for assistance from anyone to deal with any impossible pressure. God will see you through by your lonesome. Otherwise you will be weak and irresponsible."

She had no freedom to choose how to deal with oppressive situations. She had never seen that she had the alternative to opt out of a situation as a responsible method of coping. When she realized with her counselor's help the folly of her secular scripture, she was able to choose to drop the course and experienced a deep sense of relief. When pastoral counselors help people confront their idolatry and their secular scriptures, counselees may be liberated from their bondage to justification by good works and may be receptive to the realm of Divine grace.

Occasionally, a pastoral counselor may find that some individuals who are focused on the burdensome, worrisome dimensions of life to the exclusion of experiences of grace may be able to expand their horizons by encountering some revelatory event in

God's creation. A touching illustration of how a person struggling with burdens and darkness came open to the light of grace occurred in Boston at the time of the Bicentennial, when the tall ships were visiting the city. A counselee with a poetic spirit tells of her experience at that time:

"The tall ships were coming to Boston. Television, newspapers, magazines, the radio announced them. Images of the ships persisted in breaking into my consciousness. Sophistication failed me. I found myself drawn into the excitement their beauty evoked. The day the ships sailed into Boston Harbor I sat in our dining room unable to mobilize myself to do anything but become increasingly aware that I needed to see a tall ship. The intensity of the need frightened me. I did not understand it or the tears which burned behind my eyes and would not come.

"The next day I shared with my counselor the previous day's experience. I was struggling with much self doubt and such uncertainties about my worth and abilities. But I was also drawn mysteriously to the visit of the tall ships. It was so simple. The counselor suggested, 'Why don't you go to Boston Harbor this week? Spend time on a tall ship. Use all of your senses to experience it. Be open to whatever the tall ships are trying to say to you. Then, reflect and write as you see fit.'

"I did. With 250,000 other Bostonians that Wednesday I stood in line moving around the pier until I reached the *Sagres II* from Portugal. Upon boarding the ship everything and every-body around me disappeared. For an hour I allowed the ship to take shape within me. For two days after, its image remained solidified within me. On the third day it moved and I wrote:

"I am a TALL SHIP, majestic, beautiful and centered.
I am GRACE. I feel the wind filling my sails, empowering me.
I AM NOT AFRAID.

For even as I move I hold my center.
It keeps me to a steady course
as I feel moving beneath me the currents which would deny me any destination.
as I feel the water's movement; some days a caress,
rocking me, supporting me, embracing me.
other days my enemy; attacking, pounding, washing over me.

I WAIT. I LISTEN.

The sea calms. The air stills.
I feel my pain but I AM afloat.
And the promise of another breeze is all around me.
It stirs. I must prepare.

I am aware of those parts of me which give
   strength and beauty
      that are a part of my design
         without which I would fall
            the ropes
               the rigging
               the mast
                  the wheel
                     the anchor
all holding each other in perfect tension
each requiring a special discipline to function.
How my sails swell to catch the wind
   when those parts in a symphony
      of timing and precision
         MOVE.

I AM FREE!"

Another way in which people come to grips with
the need to be their own savior is through
encountering Jesus in contemplative prayer on
scriptural events. Placing oneself existentially into
various biblical scenes and acting out in imagination
the different roles, including speaking with the
principals of the story, may not only disclose the
extent to which one has needed to be one's own
savior but may also open up the possibilities of
trusting in God's love. Sometimes this process may
be carried out in spiritual direction. For example,
when people in spiritual direction go through a
period in which they are emotionally or spiritually
immobilized, the director may suggest prayerful

involvement in the story of the paralytic brought to Jesus by four friends and let down through the roof for healing. It is not uncommon that the individuals are able to identify with the paralytic, but cannot allow themselves to be dependent, in imagination, on friends for help in overcoming the crowded conditions near Jesus. People may get a deeper sense of what it means to live by the conviction "I'd rather do it myself" when they see how they resist allowing the caring of friends that makes it possible for help to take place.

Another example that I personally experienced in spiritual direction occurred when my director recommended contemplative prayer concerning Jesus washing the disciples' feet on the evening of the Last Supper. When the director suggested the footwashing account, my initial thought was, "Of course it would be easy for me to wash another's feet." But then I suddenly realized that in suggesting that particular passage the director intended for me not to *do* the footwashing but to *receive* it. I struggled with that passage for weeks, trying to let myself give up being the helper for being the recipient of the footwashing ministry.

The theme of justification by works can also be seen at times in dreams. A client had the following dream in which one of the themes was finding acceptance through capably and competently serving others. The client dreamed she was in her apartment with a woman friend when other people, including her boss, came to visit. The boss's legs were in braces, reminding the client of the time she also had worn a brace. These people stayed all night, and the next morning they went to church. The service was very long, and the client fell asleep during the prayer. They did not leave church until after one o'clock. When they returned to the client's apartment, the potatoes which had been planned for dinner were rotten. The people said they wouldn't eat and left; then the client felt very lonely.

After this dream was shared in a therapy group, someone responded, "So you were left all alone with your rotten potatoes." She replied, "I was just exhausted in trying to make them comfortable. I was so busy, just like when my family comes and I worry about making them comfortable." She had been so busy trying to make her guests feel comfortable that she was exhausted and could not really stay awake during the church service. Another person in the group asked her, "What do you think Jesus would say about the dream?" She quickly responded, "You know, the dream reminded me of Mary and Martha." Through understanding the wisdom in the dream, she came to realize how busy she was trying to work out acceptance by others, including God, through performing exhausting tasks. She had missed the one thing needful of receiving and enjoying the relationship of love and grace with her Divine Friend.

One of my most moving experiences involving dream work on the theme of justification came while leading a therapy group. The presenter of the dream had a great deal of hurt and rejection in her background, and she had assumed a parental role in her relationships. It was difficult for her to rely upon people or God in her life. But there came a stage in her therapy, after she had been separated from her husband, when overwhelming stress had literally forced her to depend upon the group, including the therapist. She had the following dream at this time.

She was tied with three other women to a raft. She was cold and hungry, but she could do nothing to work out a rescue for herself in the ocean. One of the women cried out that they wouldn't be rescued, but suddenly a Coast Guard boat appeared with myself at the helm. I connected the raft to the boat and pulled the raft toward the shore. Once in shallow water, I untied the women and they were safe. The client, however, was irritated because she had not been untied earlier and then immediately pulled into the boat, where it would have been dry and there would have been food. But then she discovered that all of the women had been tied together by a single rope and that if the rope had been cut or loosened in deep water, one or all of them might have drowned. She also realized that she could not swim. The way the client would have arranged her rescue would probably have led to her being drowned and lost. It was only in giving up her usual controls and trusting in others that she was able to be rescued. Thus there was a method of rescue which seemed to come from beyond herself, quite different from her traditional strategy of total self-reliance.

Confrontation utilizing pastoral authority to

identify as idolatry the client's sanctified pattern of justification by works is occasionally useful in liberating people to live by faith instead of works.

For example, an active churchwoman had grown up in a family where niceness, sweetness, and goodness were absolute necessities for emotional survival. This client, however, had transferred this pattern to her larger world. She clearly identified being nice with being saintly. With a clear understanding of her dynamics and a solid rapport in the relationship, I challenged her from a theological point of view to consider that earning her points for sainthood by being so sweet and nice was idolatrous in terms of justification by merit. I also suggested that her saintliness had much more to do with the demonic than it did with the Divine. While the confrontation was a radical challenge to her fundamental orientation in life, she was able to grasp that her soul was in danger if she continued with the deceptive defensive strategy of trying to save herself by her saintly niceness.

The essence of pastoral psychotherapy in regard to this theme of helping persons to move from the old creation of self-justification to the new creation in which we are justified by faith through grace is well said in these words from Ephesians:

> But even though we were dead in our sins, God, who is rich in mercy, because of the great love he had for us, gave us life together with Christ—it is, remember, by grace and not by achievement that you are saved—and has lifted us right out of the old life to take our place with him in Christ Jesus in the Heavens.

Thus he shows for all the ages to come the tremendous generosity of the grace and kindness he has expressed towards us in Christ Jesus. For it is by grace that you are saved, through faith. This does not depend on anything you have achieved, it is the free gift of God; and because it is not earned no man can boast about it. For God has made us what we are, created in Christ Jesus to do those good deeds which he planned for us to do (Eph. 2:4-10 JBP).

The Incarnational Ministry

A familiar story concerns a little girl named Maria. Her mother was a devout, religious woman, who was trying to raise Maria with a sense of love and acceptance. She didn't want Maria to be a fearful person. The essence of the mother's teachings to Maria was, "God loves you; God will guide you; God will protect you. You never have to be afraid." But one night there was a terrible thunderstorm. Maria was in her bedroom by herself. She had her nose pressed to the windowpane, watching the lightning zigzag through the sky and listening to the crashing of thunder. "Mommy, Mommy, I'm scared," she cried out. Her mother came to the door of Maria's room and said, "Now, Maria, haven't I taught you that God loves you and protects you and you never have to be afraid of anything?" "I know, Mommy, I believe all that. But tonight I need someone with skin on."

The ministry of pastoral counseling is for people

who need someone with skin on. It is an incarnational ministry. It is a ministry of journeying with persons through their fearful storms and their dark days. It is a walking into the hells of people's inner lives, of their conflicted interpersonal relationships, as well as into hellholes of social oppression and injustice. To journey into the hells of those who come to us for help we need to know in our own hearts and souls that the caring, suffering love of God has been there before us in those hellish places, is there with us now, and will be there after we leave. One major Protestant book of worship has a footnote to the Apostles' Creed noting an optional phrase: "Traditional use of this creed includes these words: 'He descended into hell.' "[1] My gut response is, Hell, that phrase is not optional! The living knowledge that God is intimately involved in the pain and struggles of all people is a guiding metaphor for our courageous commitment to minister in the dark and shadowy places of human life.

Wounded Healers

I am convinced that it is only as pastoral counselors come to grips again and again with the pain, hurt, vulnerability, and hells of their own lives that they can more fully minister to the sufferings of others. Henri Nouwen's concept of the wounded healer is an appropriate image here.[2] The quality of pastoral counseling is often determined by whether a counselor has faced his or her own emotional and spiritual wounds and has found healing and comfort. Avoiding and denying the task of seeking redemption from pain may create serious barriers to effective functioning for a pastoral counselor. Too many pastoral counselors react as I did when informed by my doctoral advisor that it was a necessary part of my academic program to be involved in my own didactic therapy. I felt betrayed and angry about this, because I had not entered the program with any understanding that such a personal investigation of my psyche was part of my academic contract. Needless to say, my sophomoric blindness to my unconscious problems was soon overcome, as the tip of my psychic iceberg emerged, and years of therapy with various therapists brought transformations and healing.

It became painfully evident to me that knowing the skills of pastoral counseling was not enough. The main instrument in the art of pastoral counseling, my own self, needed to be explored and transformed if my own wounds and blind spots were not to adversely affect the persons I was seeing in counseling. How often do we, as pastoral counselors, respond with understanding, compassion, and creative coping strategies because we have gone through the same struggles that our clients are describing to us? This is akin to a counselor and a client parachuting from an airplane into a jungle. When they land, the counselor is able to be a guide for the client because the counselor has had previous experience in exploring his or her own inner jungle as well as having guided others through their jungles.

This truth was demonstrated in a doctoral research study involving clergy some years ago.[3] These clergy went through a thirteen-week seminar which focused on their ministry to the bereaved. The seminar taught the clergy the knowledge and best skills for helping those going through the grief process. They were pre-tested to ascertain their level of effectiveness in their ministry to the bereaved before the seminar began. Immediately following the thirteen-week seminar, the same test was given to see what impact the seminar had had on participants. The post-test indicated substantial growth in the pastors' skills in ministering to the bereaved. Months later the same test was administered again to check out the lasting effects of the seminar. The results were disappointing; during the period since the conclusion of the seminar the clergy had regressed to their former level of effectiveness in coping with grief situations.

A major reason for the regression was probably that the participating clergy were not asked during the seminar to address their own experiences of grief and loss. Since these wounded healers had not worked directly with their own pain and sadness, nor were their own personal attitudes and values regarding grief dealt with in the seminar, they had not really integrated the new information for any long-term transformation. There is a profound sense in which the ministry of pastoral counseling is centered in the very heart of the pastoral counselor. "The mind is in the heart" is a way of stating the critical truth of the therapeutic use of self in the ministry of pastoral counseling.

The pastoral counselor's intrinsic world view and belief system have a profound impact on counseling relationships. The experiences which have helped shape the values, attitudes, object relations, conscious and unconscious mental representations of God, and beliefs of the pastoral counselor play a powerful role in either promoting growth or adding barriers to creativity and development.

I was particularly struck with the impact of clergy operational theologies on people during the time I served as a missionary in the Philippines. Early Protestant missionary attitudes and values regarding the grief process were that the expression of sadness in the face of a loved one's death was a sign of a lack of faith and of being a weak Christian. The natural sadness over death induced a lot of guilt in church people, and they felt their sadness was an expression of unfaith and unbelief. Such guilt compounded their difficulties in working through the grief experience. A whole sub-culture within the Philippine Protestant church internalized a counter scripture to, "Blessed are they that mourn, for they shall be comforted," which read something like, "Blessed are those who witness to their faith by not being sad in the face of the death of loved ones." In similar ways the pastoral counselor's belief system in regard to experiences of grief, guilt, anger, anxiety, sexuality, et cetera, has a profound influence upon counselees.

Pastoral counseling is fundamentally "an encounter between the gods." The field of interaction between the pastoral counselor and clients represents an arena in which the world views, value systems, belief systems, idolatries, false gods, and the true God all intersect. While some therapists still proclaim the importance of the neutrality of the therapist, most pastoral counselors are enlightened enough to believe that their own operational theology, world views, and belief systems are communicated at least unconsciously to their clients. Paul Tournier has particularly noted the spiritual and ethical influence therapists have with their clients, whether it is exerted consciously or unconsciously, intentionally or unintentionally. Tournier writes:

> Psychoanalysts sometimes reproach me for not maintaining the moral neutrality, which they consider to be the basic principle to the exercise of their vocation, because I do not hide my convictions. I am in full agreement with them when they say that psychotherapy ought to be non-directive. I think I take as much care as they to avoid the "sermon," moral exhortation and advice. But who can claim to be really morally neutral? No one, in my opinion—neither they nor I. We can indeed watch that we say nothing openly that might betray our secret reflections and judgments, but they are nonetheless there, and do not escape our patients' intuition.[4]

So there is a witness to one's world view, operational theology, belief system, and values in the process of doing pastoral counseling.

In emphasizing the significance of the therapeutic use of the pastoral counselor's personality and the impact of that counselor's operational theology, it is imperative to note that one does not have to have all of one's wounds healed or all of the demons transformed before one can minister to other people. But one needs to be in pilgrimage in exploring and experiencing the redemption of the shadowy parts of one's own life if one is to evolve an effective ministry of pastoral counseling. A unique way of stating that one does not let the counter-transference of one's unhealthy operational theology negatively impact on one's counselees is Peter Taylor Forsyth's pithy phrase, "he shall not make his myopia the standard of vision."[5]

The pastoral counselor needs through various means of contemplation, whether in supervision, personal therapy, journal writing, meditation, or prayer, to keep reaching for the deep inner authenticity of the true self. One needs to keep open to the unfolding of one's genuine identity which is fully discovered in relationship to the Identity in whose image all of us are created. A Hasidic tale exposes how long the journey often takes to find this kind of soul treasure deep within oneself.

The story is told of a rabbi named Isaac, son of Yekel, who lived in Cracow. This elderly and somewhat sickly rabbi had a dream which repeated itself three times. In the dream there was a treasure buried under the bridge leading up to the castle in Prague. After having the dream for the third time, Rabbi Isaac decided that he would take his cane and set out on foot for the long journey to Prague. When he arrived in Prague, weary and exhausted, he was disappointed to discover that the bridge leading up to the palace was guarded day and night. He could not figure out any way to explore for the treasure which his dream had indicated was buried under the bridge.

As he wandered around that area pondering what he should do, the captain of the guard noticed the elderly rabbi, and asked him what he was doing there. The rabbi told him of his recurring dream of the treasure buried underneath the bridge leading up to the palace. The captain of the guard laughed and said, "Foolish man. Some years ago I had a dream of a treasure buried in Cracow. The treasure was hidden underneath the stove of a man named Isaac, son of Yekel. Probably half of the people in Cracow are named Isaac, and the other half are named Yekel. It's ridiculous to follow your dreams." The rabbi smiled, turned, and began the long journey back to his home in Cracow. When he arrived at his own little house, he went and dug beneath the stove. There he discovered a treasure, and with the money built himself a house of prayer.

Barriers to Grace Derived from the Pastoral Counselor's Family of Origin

Pastoral counselors are often blocked in experiencing that they are beloved children of God because the quality of interpersonal relationships in their families of origin kept them from enjoying the child-self or child ego state of healthy dependency.

For reasons of emotional survival in the family of origin, they abandoned the child-self and developed a reaction formation of messianic parenthood to their families; they tend to repeat that same script and same savior role throughout life. Having read over five hundred family of origin papers written by seminarians, I believe that at least 95 percent of those going into ministry have had substantial hurt, problems, and struggles in the formative years. The object relations established in those early years and the development of the mental representations of God obviously leave those individuals with distorted world views and with operational theologies that are clearly quite different from the gospel of the good news in Jesus Christ.

Without corrective emotional experiences or the therapeutic interventions of significant others into their lives, the person will unconsciously repeat in adulthood the role of the strong, giving, ministering one with the starving child-self hidden deep within. Such a person is often conditioned to be afraid of grace and being ministered unto because she or he has found trust only in her or himself and not in significant others. Such a pattern tends to block openness to the experience of Jesus Christ as ultimate authority and Lord and as the accepting Savior and rescuer, since one has learned to be one's own master and to develop one's own strategies for salvation through justification by overt and covert good works. Karen Horney speaks of this defensive pattern as the "neurotic glory" which masks the basic anxiety of the hidden and hurting inner child-self.[6] Pastoral counselors caught in this pattern need to come to grips with the unresolved hang-ups of their "inner child of the past."[7]

I believe that the most common countertransference problem for pastoral counselors, emerging from their family histories, is the tendency to be the rescuing savior, the Christ, the redeemer, and the loving messiah. Igor Caruso writes:

> It seems to me that countertransference in connection with the "Christ-archetype" can be still more active (and maybe still more dangerous) than the countertransference of other complexes on the part of the analyst, for instance any sexual complexes. . . . We believe that the so-called training analysis should not merely serve to make the future analyst conscious of, say, his sexual complexes, but also—especially in its constructive aspect of existential synthesis—to crystallize this identity towards redeeming and being redeemed. If the analyst simply "analyzes away" or disowns the "Christ-archetype" within himself, he will court danger both to his patients and himself. It may easily happen that he may be dominated by the redeemer part, but this will remain immanent, and it will be transferred unconsciously, in a fallacious manner, to the patient's personality.

> Moreover, every patient projects on to his analyst a nebulous idea somewhat on the following lines: The healer is bound to identify himself with the person in search of healing; he has to sacrifice himself and take on the burden of neurosis in order to be able to descend with the neurotic into the hell of the neurosis

and to rise with him again. It is of little use for the analyst to think that this unclear sacrificial process is in fact impossible. If the analyst has no support in the conscious cleansing of the "Christ-archetype," he is in danger of becoming fascinated in his own role as redeemer. The psychoanalyst's terrible temptation, which is not made any easier by the fact that in most cases it remains unconscious, is to become God and play Christ. On the other hand, the psychoanalyst, led by the "Christ-archetype," has to be healer and "redeemer." Unless his inner life thus corresponds to this vocation, he will be a false redeemer.[8]

Likewise, Ana-Maria Rizzuto has raised the curious question that if the mental representation of God is so critical to emotional balance regarding a person's mental health, then it is amazing that analysts have not looked at their own mental representations of God in their didactic analysis. She writes:

> In their training our generation of analysts have not received the detailed understanding I think is neces- sary to appreciate the specific contribution of the God representation to psychic balance. As in many other areas, if the analyst's personal analysis has not helped him come to terms with his religious beliefs or lack of them, there is risk of unchecked countertransference reactions in this realm.[9]

The pastoral counselor's vocational role as a false Christ is helpful to clients, up to a point. Such a counselor may help the counselee to become liberated from some of the hang-ups and idolatries of the past. However, she or he may also lead a client unconsciously to a different, though one might say a higher, level of idolatry. Caruso tells an interesting story about a psychologist who had a dream indicating to him that there were messianic implications to his practice of psychotherapy.

A psychologist undergoing trainee analysis dreamed of a little shabby, ugly hairdresser in Haifa, who put a halo around his head and was convinced he was the Messiah. Analysis of this dream-content showed that the patient's efforts to cure and "redeem" people were still in flagrant contradiction with the stage of development he had actually reached. The interesting thing is that this psychologist was going through a very critical period, but had never before had any conscious misgivings reflected upon the responsibility connected with his calling. He was a prominent psychotherapist, who regarded the problems of psychotherapy as "scientific." His unconscious taught him a different lesson.[10]

The central vocational temptation and danger for the pastoral counselor is in living out the second aspect of the twin idolatry by seeking to atone for, to justify, and to save oneself by the good works of being the savior, healer, and rescuer of others. For example, the childhood role of the pastoral counselor as marital healer, family mediator, and peacemaker may be unconsciously replicated in marital and family therapy. It is not uncommon that the neophyte's hidden agenda in doing marriage and family counseling is resolution of the need to improve the parents' relationship. This may involve a covert attempt to mature and to make happier the counselees and their marriages, as surrogates of the pastoral counselor's parents and their marriage.

Unfortunately, the unconscious strategy in treating the surrogate parents' marriage does not fulfill the deep needs of the counselor's hurt child-self. Pastoral counselors may need to heal marital problems quickly because such issues may be reminiscent of the parents' marriage struggles and may resurrect childhood anxieties and the fear of parental separation. It may be painfully difficult for counselors to allow a couple to explore their conflicts, their resistance to change, and the satisfactions of maintaining a conflictive relationship.

A graphic example of this occurred in a supervisory session with a pastoral counselor who was counseling a minister and his wife in conjoint marital therapy. The minister was struggling with his ambivalence about the marriage, and he discussed a number of times his need to get away from his wife for a period of time to reflect on their relationship. Each time the husband pressed his need for some distance, the counselor increased his efforts to hold the couple together and to "improve their relationship." In exploring the countertransference in this situation, the pastoral counselor's supervisor suggested that the counselor sculpt his relationship to this couple by imagining these two people seated in empty chairs facing each other and then locating himself in relationship to the couple.

In doing so, the pastoral counselor found himself standing astraddle the two chairs with an arm around each, trying to pull the partners together.

The counselor spontaneously realized that he had not been able to allow the husband the freedom to discuss his need for separateness because that activated the counselor's unresolved childhood anxiety about his parents' potential separation and the attendant fear of losing one or both of them. He had coped with that anxiety by trying to hold them together. When he realized that he was duplicating his role in his parents' marriage in the counseling relationship with this couple, he was able to give up his control and to give the husband the space necessary for exploring his separateness. When the husband no longer felt controlled and limited by the counselor, he was able to explore his needs for independence directly in the marital relationship and to deepen his sense of autonomy as well as his marital commitment, without having to leave the relationship. In the process the counselor also learned a great deal about how he was doing marital therapy on the basis of trying to rescue himself by saving the surrogate marital partners that came to him for help.

Two Life Stories

Let us look at two typical patterns demonstrating how clergy may live out their idolatrous histories in their vocational roles as minister and/or pastoral counselor. Let us take first of all an example of a parish minister and then of a specialist in pastoral counseling.

Stan Brady was a parish minister who often felt overwhelmed by congregational pressures and sometimes exhausted by never-ending parish responsibilities. Prior to therapy, Stan had no awareness of how closely his role as parish minister replicated his childhood role in his family of origin. Stan had grown up in a New England town with one older brother. He learned at an early age that it was unsafe in his home to be a vulnerable child with emotional needs. He discovered before the age of six that he needed to parent his parents and that he could not rely upon them to understand him and to meet his normal psychological and spiritual needs for affection and affirmation. His mother was a fragile person who suffered from a variety of illnesses both real and imaginary. She also was supersensitive to any slight or criticism, so that she would readily cry, get a headache, or retreat to her room if anyone displeased her in the smallest way. Stan felt that he must be her protector since his brother seemed unconcerned and selfish and his father was no comfort to her. In fact, the father tried to control the home by actual or threatened outbursts of anger, both of which Stan and his mother particularly feared.

Stan tried to be the peacemaker in his home in order to prevent conflicts between the mother and the father. Even as a pre-schooler, Stan was functioning as the caregiver, healer, and counselor to his parents so that his mother wouldn't get sick or the parents separate. The sickly, fragile mother and the critical, volatile father were in no way reliable authority figures with whom Stan could risk sharing his child-self. He had to depend on himself for survival. There was no stable love figure, no rescuer for him. In a dynamic sense Stan was functioning in various ministerial, care-giving roles in his own childhood family without having had the opportunity to be a child himself.

Stan had been overwhelmed by his responsibilities, and he carried those burdensome patterns into adulthood. In the ministry he felt trapped by the never-ending demands placed on him as a pastor; he was always trying to care for hurting people, seeking to avoid conflict in the life of the congregation, and preaching and teaching the good news when he felt weary and discouraged. He had married a non-nurturing person who added pressures by pushing him to have more children. This meant more emotional and financial responsibilities for Stan, who still had not had the experience of being a child himself. So in both his ministry and his marriage, Stan was living out his assigned childhood role of parenting everyone else while inwardly starving for love and support. While Stan's particular dynamics may differ from those of other clergy, there are nevertheless many internalized patterns repeated in adulthood and in the ministry which leave the pastor's childhood self unfulfilled and closed to receiving the good news.

The second story is about Sheila, a middle-aged client who was a nurse. She was also an active churchwoman who was articulate about her theology. Sheila had neurotic fears about the loss of

INCARNATIONAL MINISTRY

relationships, resulting from her parents' divorce and her distance from the key authority figures of her childhood. She had built her life around avoiding separation anxiety by being good, thoughtful, nice, and helpful. She had a neurotic pride in what she called her "sensitivity" to others, which made her feel saintly. She believed she had developed this sensitivity totally out of love, and she had baptized it as her finest Christian virtue. At an appropriate place in her therapy, I confronted her with the truth that her emotional radar was tuned in to others because of her fear of losing her place in the hearts of key persons in her life. I told her that it was true that she had received many strokes for her sensitivity, but that I considered her saintly pattern more demonic than divine. We discussed how this dynamic was built on an idolatrous view of the world restricting her freedom to express the assertive side of her personality. I suggested that the true God in Jesus Christ affirmed her sainthood more in the authenticity of her total humanity, including her assertiveness and her aggressiveness. God did not require her to be submissive, adaptive, sweet, and neurotically sensitive.

Her reaction to my confrontation was touching. "You really shocked me when you started to make your interpretation. I realized the tremendous risk you took in our relationship. But as you shared your perspective I became aware that you were the first person who cared enough to see through to my repressed but true self. You wanted me to be free to express the real me and to trust that it is safe enough

145

in relationships, including with God, to share that assertive part of me."

In my analysis of this confrontation, I am aware of three different ways in which the operational theology of the client and the counselor could have interfaced:

1. *A Collusion of the Gods.* The idolatrous belief systems of the client and the counselor can have such a similar configuration that their gods are in collusion and there is no opportunity for change. If I had been functioning out of fear of hurting people and of losing relationships, then I would have been too frightened of the potential conflict for the confrontation to ever take place. My ministry would have been just another benediction to her neurotic saintliness.

2. *A Direct Conflict of the Gods.* The belief systems of the client and of the counselor can be so diametrically opposed that their gods are in collision and escalating defensiveness blocks the opportunity for change. If I had been functioning out of the need to be right and to succeed in breaking through the client's defensive strategy of salvation by imposing my belief system, then conflict and further resistance would have occurred.

3. *Constructive Confrontation of the Gods.* The belief systems of the client and of the counselor are different but there is neither collusion nor collision. The counselor lovingly affirms the client's idolatrous belief system and the (once valid) need to utilize such a defensive strategy of salvation. But the counselor can also point to another reality in the Christian revelation, whereby there is a confrontation

of the God of the good news with the gods of the bad news. Utilizing my pastoral authority, I could confront Sheila with her god of separation anxiety and her false savior of sensitivity and niceness. I could testify about the God of love from whom nothing in all creation can separate and about the Savior whose love will never let us go, even in our pride, in our false selves and saintliness. I can go on caring about Sheila even if she does not affirm the theology to which I bear witness in the ministry of pastoral counseling.

Gerkin powerfully expresses his understanding of this profound role of the pastoral counselor:

> Here comes into view a fresh possibility for the analogical appropriation of incarnational theology for the ministry of pastoral care and counseling. As the Christ of the cross was the Supreme Parable of God, so we pastors may seek to become parabolic figures with those who come to us for help with their problems of historical existence. Within the parabolic imagery, our ministry becomes one of subversion, of seeking to change the mythic narratives of others' lives from the inside by the quality of our presence with them. The pastoral relationship itself should then become parabolic, giving to the narrative of the other person a new twist that opens the story to a fresh and lively possibility. Like the good parable, the pastoral relationship may be one of advent or gift, of reversal of the recipient's world, and of empowerment for action. But also in the mode of the good parable, the good pastoral relationship remains in the lower case; in its ordinariness, its human everydayness it represents and, on occasion, discloses the extraordinary—the gift of God.[11]

Supervision

A further complexity of idolatrous world views and maps of reality is seen in the supervisory process in pastoral counseling. The supervisor has to deal with his or her own operational theology as well as be aware of the maps of reality of the pastoral counselor and his or her counselee. For example, if a supervisor is dealing with a therapist and his or her client, both of whom have a world view seeing vulnerability as weak, unmasculine, or immature, then the supervisor's world view and belief system regarding these erroneous beliefs will be very important. Some supervisors may have the freedom to share their own vulnerability in the supervisory process. Others may feel comfortable in making a theological connection between their own vulnerability and the vulnerability of the love of God in the birth of the baby in the manger in Bethlehem or in the betrayal and the death upon the cross. Others may just explore the negative meanings imputed to vulnerability. If there is a collusion or a collision among the supervisor, counselor, and client, then it is unlikely that there will be a transformation in the life of the counselee or in the counseling style of the counselor.

Joy in the Ministry of Pastoral Counseling

In the ministry of pastoral counseling, while there are temptations to save oneself through seeking to be a healer for others, there is also the profound opportunity to meet the eternal Thou in I-Thou encounters with clients. While the anxiety and anguish can be great in moments of working with difficult and highly disturbed persons, there also can be the sense of being a part of the ministry of Jesus Christ which descends into the hells of human life. In those moments, a pastoral counselor knows that this is the vocation to which he or she has been called. Those sacred times of life touching life, of heart touching heart, of love touching love are beautifully humbling experiences of feeling used by the Spirit in its healing work in human life. Pastoral counselors also have the unusual opportunity to learn about themselves as they interact with their clients, who sometimes are teachers to them and prophets to them of their own shadow side.

Recently, at the conclusion of the termination process in pastoral counseling a woman gave me a parting gift of a poem by May Sarton entitled, "Death of a Psychiatrist." This poem speaks to me eloquently of the privilege we have in the counseling relationship to be the flesh that is made Word even though we may never use traditional religious language in that therapeutic process.

Death of a Psychiatrist
For Volta Hall

1

Now the long lucid listening is done,
Where shame and anguish were subtly opposed:
His patients mourn this father as their own.

Each was accepted whole and wholly known,
Down to the deepest naked need exposed.
Now the long lucid listening is done.

For the raw babe, he was a healing zone.
The cry was heard; the rage was not refused.
Each has a father to mourn as his own.

When someone sees at last, the shame is gone;
When someone hears, anguish may be composed,
And the long lucid listening is done.

The ghostly child goes forth once more alone,
And scars remain, but the deep wound is closed.
Each has a father to mourn as his own.

A guiltless loss, this shines like a sun,
And love remains, but the deep wound is closed.
Each has a father to mourn as his own,
Now the long lucid listening is done.

2

It was not listening alone, but hearing,
For he remembered every crucial word
And gave one back oneself because he heard.

Who listens so, does more than listen well.
He goes down with his patient into Hell.

It was not listening alone, but healing.
We knew a total, yet detached response,
Harsh laugh, sane and ironical at once.

Who listens so, does more than merely pity,
Restores the soul to its lost dignity.

It was not listening alone, but sharing,
And I remember how he bowed his head
Before a poem. "Read it again," he said.

Then, in the richest silence he could give,
I saw the poem born, knew it would live.

It was not listening alone, but being.
We saw a face so deeply lined and taut
It wore the passion of dispassionate thought.

Because he cared, he heard; because he heard,
He lifted, shared, and healed without a word.[12]

This psycho-spiritual ministry of pastoral counseling is an evangelical thrust of the church seeking to bring good news into the lives of those who are living according to the bad news. Pastoral counselors seek to lead people from attachments to false gods who teach them bad news about themselves to the saving knowledge of God in Christ, the true ultimate authority bearing the message of the good news. We try to help liberate people from fixations around the false centers of their lives for a singleness of mind and heart that is focused in love around the true living God.

Our task in part is carrying out the scriptural admonition which says, "Little children, keep yourselves from idols—false gods, [from anything and everything that would occupy the place in your heart due to God, from any sort of substitute for Him that would take first place in your life]" (I John 5:21 Amplified NT). This task of taking on the gods is often an arduous one, but it is also potentially joyous as people find their true selves in being related to the God who loves them into their freedom to be. Tillich challenges us with these words:

But you are supposed to pronounce and to represent the healing and demon-conquering power implied in the message of the Christ, the message of forgiveness and of a new reality. You must be conscious of the other ways of healing. You must cooperate with them, but you must not substitute them for what you represent. . . . There is no greater vocation on earth than to be called to heal and to cast out demons. Be joyous in this vocation. Do not be depressed by its burden, or even by the burden of having to deal with those who do not want to be healed. Rejoice in your calling. In spite of your own sickness, in spite of the demons working within you and your churches, you have a glimpse of what can heal ultimately, of him in Whom God made manifest his power over demons and disease, of him who represents the healing power that is in the world, and sustains the world and lifts it up to God. Rejoice in his messages. Take with you this joy.[13]

Notes

1. Pastoral Counseling as the Encounter Between Gods

1. Jane Howard, *Please Touch* (New York: McGraw-Hill, 1970), pp. 220-221.

2. Charles Gerkin, *The Living Human Document* (Nashville: Abingdon Press, 1984), p. 21.

3. Ibid., pp. 20-21, 198.

4. Lawrence E. Hedges, *Listening Perspectives in Psychotherapy* (New York: Jason Aronson, 1983).

5. Ibid., p. 1.

6. Gerkin, *Living Human Document*, p. 144.

7. Steve de Shazer and Elam Nunnelly, "The Mysterious Affair of Paradoxes and Loops," in Gerald R. Weeks, *Promoting Change Through Paradoxical Therapy* (Homewood, Ill.: Dow Jones-Irwin, 1985), p. 252.

8. Wilfried Daim, *Depth Psychology and Salvation*, trans. and ed. Kurt F. Reinhardt (New York: Ungar, 1963), p. 134, quoting Karl Jaspers.

9. J. V. Langmead Casserly, *The Christian in Philosophy* (New York: Scribner's, 1951), p. 42.

10. Earl A. Loomis, Jr., *The Self in Pilgrimage* (New York: Harper, 1960), p. 13.

11. Janet Surrey, *Self in Relation: A Theory of Women's Development* (Wellesley, Mass.: Wellesley College, The Stone Center, 02181, 1985).

12. Daim, *Depth Psychology and Salvation*, pp. 110-138.

13. Thomas Merton, *The New Man* (New York: Farrar, Straus & Giroux, 1984), p. 141.

14. Howard Thurman, *Jesus and the Disinherited* (Nashville: Abingdon-Cokesbury Press, 1949), p. 50.

15. Personal conversation with Calvin Turley, May 15, 1979.

16. Ana-Maria Rizzuto, *The Birth of the Living God* (Chicago: University of Chicago Press, 1979); John

McDargh, *Psychoanalytic Object Relations Theory and the Study of Religion* (Lanham, Md.: University Press of America, 1983). Two excellent books utilizing object relations theory as the basis for addressing the issues of the mental representations of God.

17. Wilfried Daim, "On Depth-Psychology and Salvation," *Journal of Psychotherapy as a Religious Process* 2 (January, 1955), p. 28.

18. Howard Halpern, *Cutting Loose* (New York: Bantam Books, 1978), pp. 4, 6.

19. Personal communication with Edwin A. Hoover.

20. Paul Tournier, *Guilt and Grace*, trans. Arthur W. Heathcoate (New York: Harper, 1962), p. 69.

21. Walter Brueggemann, "Covenanting as Human Vocation," *Interpretation* 33, no. 2 (1979), p. 116.

22. Daim, *Depth Psychology and Salvation*, pp. 47-51.

23. Quoted in John J. Higgins, *Thomas Merton on Prayer* (Garden City, N. Y.: Doubleday Image Books, 1975), p. 62.

24. Thomas Merton, *Bread in the Wilderness* (New York: New Directions, 1953) p. 76.

25. Ivan Boszormenyi-Nagy and Geraldine M. Spark, *Invisible Loyalties* (New York: Brunner/Mazel, 1984), p. 46.

26. Adapted case materials from work of Rachel Martin, pastoral counselor.

27. Tournier, *Guilt and Grace*, p. 69.

28. Thomas Oden, *The Structure of Awareness* (Nashville: Abingdon Press, 1969), p. 66. Fine insights about idolatry in this book.

29. Ronald D. Fairbairn, "Observations in Defense of the Object-Relations Theory of the Personality," *British Journal of Medical Psychology* 28 (1955), p. 156.

30. M. Scott Peck, M.D., *The Road Less Traveled* (New York: Simon & Schuster, 1978), p. 35.

2. It Is Easier to Ride a Camel in the Direction It Is Going

1. Carol M. Anderson and Susan Stewart, *Mastering Resistance: A Practical Guide to Family Therapy* (New York: Guilford Press, 1983), p. 23.
2. Peck, *Road Less Traveled*, pp. 46, 49.
3. Allen Fay, M.D., public lecture in New York City, 1976.
4. Virginia Satir, interviewed by Richard Simon in "Life Reaching Out to Life: A Conversation with Virginia Satir," *The Common Boundary* 3, no. 1 (1985), p. 4.
5. Milton Erikson and Ernest Rossi, "Varieties of Double Bind," *The American Journal of Clinical Hypnosis* 17 (1975) p. 143.
6. Allen Fay, M. D., *Making Things Better by Making Them Worse* (New York: Hawthorn Books, 1978), pp. 25-26.
7. Harold Greenwald, "Direct Decision Therapy," *Voices* 7, no. 1 (Spring 1971).
8. Anderson and Stewart, *Mastering Resistance*, p. 8.

3. The Implicit Religious Drama in Marital and Family Counseling

1. Eric Berne, *A Layman's Guide to Psychiatry and Psychoanalysis* (New York: Grove Press, 1957), p. 16.
2. Robert Stahmann and William Hiebert, *Premarital Counseling* (Lexington, Mass.: Heath Books, 1981). An excellent discussion can be found here of meeting with families of origin in premarital counseling.
3. Tournier, *Guilt and Grace*, p. 167.
4. Maurice Freedman, *The Healing Dialogue in Psychotherapy* (New York: Jason Aronson, 1985), p. 123.
5. Carl Rogers, *A Way of Being* (Boston: Houghton Mifflin, 1980), p. 23.

6. A. H. Maslow and Bela Mittelman, *Principles of Abnormal Psychology* (New York: Harper, 1941), p. 6.

4. The Operational Theology of the "Common Cold"—Depression

1. Søren Kierkegaard, *Purity of Heart Is to Will One Thing*, trans. Douglas Steere (New York: Harper, 1956), p. 169.

2. James L. Muyskens, *The Sufficiency of Hope* (Philadelphia: Temple University Press, 1979), p. 130.

3. David D. Burns, M.D., *Feeling Good: The New Mood Therapy* (New York: William Morrow, 1980), p. 21.

4. Burns, *Feeling Good*, p. 39.

5. Howard Thurman, *Meditations of the Heart* (New York: Harper, 1953), p. 36.

6. Friedrich Nietzsche, *Human, All Too Human: A Book for Free Spirits*, vol. 1, trans. Helen Zimmern (New York: Gordon Press, 1974), p. 82.

7. Percy Bysshe Shelley, *The Cenci*.

8. Søren Kierkegaard, *The Sickness Unto Death* (Garden City, N.Y.: Doubleday, 1954), p. 241.

9. Ibid., p. 240.

10. Paul W. Pruyser, "Anxiety: Affect or Cognitive State," in Seward Hiltner and Karl Menninger, eds., *Constructive Aspects of Anxiety* (Nashville : Abingdon Press, 1963), pp. 137, 138.

11. Helmut Thielicke, *Between God and Satan*, trans. C. C. Barber (Grand Rapids, Mich.: Wm. B. Eerdmans, 1958), p. 6.

12. Thomas Merton, *Seeds of Contemplation* (New York: Dell, 1949), pp. 102-103.

13. Daim, *Depth Psychology and Salvation*, p. 59.

14. Helmut Thielicke, *Nihilism*, trans. John W. Doberstein (New York: Harper, 1961), p. 13.

15. Ibid., p. 146.

5. Self-justification Versus Justification by Faith Through Grace

1. Le Roy Aden, "Pastoral Counseling and Self-Justification," *Journal of Psychology and Christianity* 3, no. 4 (Winter 1984), p. 23.

2. C. R. Snyder, Raymond L. Higgins, and Rita J. Stucky, *Excuses: Masquerades in Search of Grace* (New York: John Wiley, 1983), p. 28.

3. Paul J. Tillich, *The Impact of Psychotherapy on Theological Thought*, Monograph of the Academy of Religion and Mental Health, (1960), pp. 4, 5.

4. Reuel L. Howe, *Man's Need and God's Action* (Greenwich, Conn.: Seabury Press, 1953), p. 42.

6. The Incarnational Ministry

1. The United Methodist Church, *The Book of Worship for Church and Home* (Nashville, Tenn.: The United Methodist Publishing House, 1964), p. 179.

2. Henri J. M. Nouwen, *The Wounded Healer* (Garden City, N.Y.: Doubleday, 1972).

3. Donovan Hommen, "An Assessment of the Effects of a Laboratory-Training-Education Program in Bereavement Ministry Conducted by a Community Mental Health Center for Parish Clergymen," (Ph.D. diss., Boston University, 1972).

4. Paul Tournier, *A Place for You* (Richmond, Va.: John Knox Press, 1965), p. 85.

5. Peter Taylor Forsyth, *Positive Preaching and the Modern Mind* (London: Independent Press, 1907) p. 236.

6. Karen Horney, *Neurosis and Human Growth* (New York: W. W. Norton, 1950), pp. 23-27.

7. W. Hugh Missildine, *Your Inner Child of the Past* (New York: Simon & Schuster, 1963).

8. Igor Caruso, *Existential Psychology*, trans. Eva Krapf (Great Britain: Herder and Herder, 1964), pp. 164-172.

9. Rizzuto, *Birth of the Living God*, p. 210.

10. Caruso, *Existential Psychology*, p. 170.

11. Gerkin, *Living Human Document*, p. 176.

12. May Sarton, "Death of a Psychiatrist," *A Private Mythology* (New York: W. W. Norton, 1966), pp. 97-98.

13. Paul Tillich, *The Eternal Now* (New York: Scribner's, 1963), pp. 64, 65.